SHOW RUNNER

SHOW RUNNER

PRODUCING VARIETY AND TALK SHOWS FOR TELEVISION

STEVE CLEMENTS

SILMAN-JAMES PRESS   LOS ANGELES

First Edition
10 9 8 7 6 5 4 3 2 1

Library of Congress Cataloging-in-Publication Data

Cover design by

Printed and bound in the United States of America

Silman-James Press
1181 Angelo Drive
Beverly Hills, CA 90210

This book is dedicated to my wife, Claudia Coplon Clements.
Meeting her in time to spend the second half of my life with her
was the luckiest break I've ever had. She is my best friend,
loving companion—and my exceptionally talented editor.
Fade up on the best years ahead.

CONTENTS

PREFACE

THE JOYS OF PRODUCING

I always enjoyed looking into the eyes of people who asked what type of work I did. My answer was simple: "I'm a television producer."

That was when the fun began. Their eyes would narrow with distrust and then widen with excitement that my answer was, just possibly, true. That's when a cross-examination would begin to determine whether I was a liar, a "wannabe," or an actual television producer whom they had "the good fortune" to meet on this particular day.

Their next question was inevitably, "Have you produced any shows I would know?" Rather than rudely respond, "I have no idea which shows you would know," I would politely rattle off the names of several shows I had produced—only the successful ones, of course. The excitement of the listener grew. "*You* did that show?" Then came the inevitable, "So what does a producer do?"

"What does a producer do?" is the eternal question, and I could not do the answer justice in quick cocktail conversation situations. I always tried to tell them a little but, when their eyes glazed over, I switched to telling them about the excitement I felt as a producer. And, of course, I told them a bit of my personal history. I told them how blood pulsed through my veins every morning because I couldn't wait to get to work. I even got to bring my work home: I did *pre-interviews*—interviews with guests to determine subjects for Dinah Shore to discuss and to formulate the anecdotes that would be told. I even told them about being called from the house while grilling on the barbeque. "Steve, Sylvester Stallone for you." Now *that* was show business!

Who would have thought this possible when, as a three-year-old in Brooklyn, New York, the highlight of each of my days was watching television programs on my godmother's flickering black-and-white ten-inch screen? At 5:30 every evening, I would walk upstairs from our basement apartment into her house to watch *Howdy Doody* since we couldn't afford our own TV. As the years went on, I remained to watch the news with anchor John Cameron Swayze, who instilled in me a never-abating interest in current events. After the news were the fifteen-minute variety shows hosted by Perry Como, Jo Stafford, and Dinah Shore. Although my fantasies about appearing on and "making TV shows"—I didn't know the term producer then—began at this young age, it is still an amazing irony that the first famous television personality for whom I wrote nearly thirty years later was the very same Dinah Shore! Since I had been warned that she was particularly sensitive about her age, I never found the right way to tell her that this thirty-plus-year-old man had been her fan since he was three. I would never have believed that she and I would one day sit together planning and scripting nearly 200 of her daily ninety-minute programs.

When I was eight years old, my parents took me to see my first live television broadcast—*The Milton Berle Show*. As I sat in the audience watching Berle with his guests (I can't believe I remember this), Cesar Romero and Kathryn Murray, I wanted to jump onstage and take part —not necessarily as the star, but as one of the people involved in what was happening up there. In those early days it was nearly impossible to see the show itself because of the lighting instruments hanging down over the stage. The audience had to bend down to peer under these klieg lights. Even with these difficulties, I was excited to be in the audience because I realized that everything I was watching in the studio was being seen by millions of people at that very moment! The high I derived from that concept was the essence of my drive to become part of a medium that could reach an entire nation from a single television studio in Manhattan.

Although my parents seemed to enjoy my rapture for live television, they did not realize until later the two negative effects it would have on them—one, they would be asked to escort me to any and every television show with a studio audience, and two, any hopes they had of my becoming a doctor were now dashed. As the years passed, I dragged them not only to classic shows with Jackie Gleason, Ed Sullivan, and a one-time-only New York broadcast by one of my heroes who was based in Hollywood, Jack Benny, but also to a slew of inane game shows, such as *The Big Payoff*.

These days bring to mind my first television-producing lesson—what seems to be spontaneous on television is usually prepared in advance. Further, it is not what it seems to be. During an episode of the game show *Strike It Rich,* the host, Warren Hull, was looking for "someone, anyone from the studio audience" who would be able to answer the questions for a contestant who spoke only Italian. When Hull, supposedly, randomly selected a man sitting on an aisle about four rows back, I was horrified to see that the selected audience member was already wearing pancake makeup. I remember thinking what a hoax it was. Ironically, the quiz show scandals of the late 1950s confirmed that pre-selecting a contestant from the audience was just the "tip of the iceberg" when it came to manipulating the content of a television show. Who were the major culprits? Who committed what became known as one of the biggest rip-offs in the history of the industry? It was the producers, Jack Barry and Dan Enright. The producers!

From the moment I was able to read, I devoured everything that was printed about television. By age six, besides enjoying reading gossip about celebrities in magazines and newspapers, I began to read the show business "bible," *Variety.* My favorite day of the week was Wednesday. That was the day both *TV Guide* and *Variety* were published. I picked them up from a small neighborhood magazine and sundries store known as a "candy store" in Brooklyn. A half century later I still read *Variety* but, instead of the weekly version, I read the daily one published in Hollywood. I was fascinated by programming strategy; I studied ratings and relished all analyses of why certain shows worked while others were doomed to failure.

As I attended more and more television broadcasts—mostly tapings after 1958, and finally without my parents, who never attended a taping again until I was a producer myself—I was continually amazed by the dozens of people who worked together with the precision of dancers in a choreographed piece. The camera people knew just when to move in and then back out as the big crane camera rose to its greatest height to create a kaleidoscope effect with Jackie Gleason's June Taylor dancers. I had the opportunity to sit in the control room of a show called *Odyssey,* watching and listening in fascination as the director yelled instructions into a microphone to the personnel onstage and in the control room. I wanted to know who each person in the control booth and the studio was—who did what to make the show happen and, most of all, how to sign up to become a part of this exciting world.

Given my knowledge, my love for the medium, and my drive to succeed, it would seem logical that I would have begun my television career right after graduating from college. However, as the son of an artist who had barely weathered the Depression, I was coaxed into teaching high school and then college while I pursued advanced degrees. It was not until a decade following graduation after earning several minor credits in theater and television that I finally moved to Hollywood to pursue the dream I had had since I was a child.

I was fortunate to have almost immediate success as a sitcom writer for *Welcome Back, Kotter* and *Three's Company*, but found the work tiresome. I was always working with a partner in one of our apartments, counting down the time until I could go to lunch. After a meeting with the staff producers and writers, we would rewrite, and then do more rewrites. I didn't feel that I was in "show business." I felt as though I had an office job.

Finally when the opportunity came to become a full-time writer for my childhood heroine, Dinah Shore, it changed my life. I was to be one of four writers for her daily ninety-minute music-comedy-talk show. This show would offer me the opportunity to do everything I had always longed to do in a studio facility I often passed, never believing that I would have the opportunity to work there.

In three days every week we taped a total of six shows at CBS Television City in Hollywood.

There were dozens of people in the production—researchers who supplied the writers with information about the celebrities and *talent coordinators* who booked those celebrities. The coordinators crowed with pride whenever they made a blue index card: This blue card announced that the particular coordinator had secured a coveted star that was a *"tough get."* A "tough get" is talent coordinator parlance for anyone who rarely does talk shows. Of course, if that guest canceled, the talent coordinator would quietly sneak to the "booking board" and remove the card, hoping that no one remembered it was ever there. There were also secretaries and production assistants who did a variety of tasks, including clearing the rights for every piece of music used in the show. Deals had to be struck regarding price, even if the notes were just "tinkled" on the piano for a moment or two. There was even a musical director who wrote special material for Dinah and worked with her daily to maximize a voice that was starting to lose its luster.

I loved going onstage to chat with the four cameramen and enjoy the comic antics of the stage manager, who used his acting background to make everyone laugh and relax while making sure everyone did their jobs. He also had to give all time cues to Dinah based on those given to him from the control room.

After the final rehearsal to set camera positions for all the demonstration segments and musical numbers, the writers would meet with Dinah in her dressing room, as she became transformed from an attractive sixtyish woman into the glamorous and ageless Dinah Shore who received huge ovations when she was introduced to the audience. Even on the days when she seemed depressed and was dealing with personal problems, she would light up, laugh, and joke with the audience as announcer Johnny Gilbert said, "Ladies and gentlemen, Miss Dinah Shore." I got chills watching the low-key woman I had just *briefed* in the dressing room—preparing her for the questions and expected answers from each guest—become the legendary television star.

Before some tapings, life was frenetic. If Dinah changed much of the script, the other writers and I had to give all changes to the cue card guys. Sometimes there were literally seconds between the time the changes were made and the moment Dinah read those lines. I trembled when I thought of what might happen if the cue card guy didn't make it onstage and Dinah found no card when she needed it.

Some of you must have read the last few paragraphs and said to yourselves, "Why would anyone want to do that?" Others, like me, thrive on the challenge, the action, and the adrenaline. I was now one of the people I had watched at the live broadcasts and tapings throughout my youth. I was Walter Mitty living out his personal daydream and I was being paid for it—and paid well! Of course, as I learned more about how this type of show went from concept to tape, I wanted to do more than write. I wanted to be the producer of non-fiction shows—the person whose dreams could be realized on the small screen.

For those of you who, after reading this book, decide to be engineers or lawyers, I understand completely and wish you well in your chosen fields. For those who wish for constant adrenaline rushes, opportunities to meet and work with big stars and world leaders, and the possibility to become part of a large, sociable team with a common goal, remember this section. To achieve your goal of becoming a producer, you will encounter many speed bumps along the way. My purpose in writing this book is not to make these bumps larger than they actually are, nor shield you from the realities of the business. Instead, I hope you will gain the knowledge from this book to make your road to the top filled with as few surprises as possible.

If you do decide that this is the field for you, you will be entering it with more inside information than I had, despite my years of reading *Variety* and, as a result, with a tremendous advantage.

INTRODUCTION

I like to think of this book as a written documentary. As you leaf through these pages whether as a student, prospective producer, or interested layperson, I hope you will sense my panic as a producer when a guest dropped out at the last minute, feel the gnawing in the pit of my stomach when the ratings were sinking fast, or share my exhilaration at doing a good broadcast. For those students who are using this as a textbook, I have italicized pertinent terminology. Along with the definitions within the text, there is an index that references the page on which each word is defined.

If the experience begun here continues for you onto the show *floor*—used professionally rather than stage—the overriding rule to govern yourself is "go with the flow." Keep calm, marshal your forces, and strive for positive results.

During the nearly quarter century I was a national television producer, I vied with my peers for the same positions. We all knew one another, almost as classmates do. We would wave during interviews for jobs, gritting our teeth that "so and so" could even be considered for the same gig. We were in constant competition for any opportunity to produce a daytime magazine, one-subject talk, variety, talk-variety, late-night magazine, game, or cable children's shows, all of which, in "televisionglese," fall under the heading of non-fiction television.

Why does non-fiction television cut such a broad swath? Non-fiction television is supposed to be synonymous with reality, as opposed to the fantasy of a sitcom, made-for-television movie, or one-hour drama. It's hard to believe that a variety show could share the same non-fiction genre as a cable children's show, the news, game shows, and the "real TV" shows that emerged in the late 1990s. As for reality, anyone who watches television has to wonder occasionally whether some of the medium's so-called real TV shows even come close to reality. Between extreme dating, extreme makeovers, extreme love affairs, and extreme sports, reality seems to be stretched beyond, well, extreme.

The discriminating difference is that non-fiction shows are not fully scripted, as situation comedies or dramatic series are. The same is true for talk shows, even though portions of these are scripted and on TelePrompTer. Variety shows fit into the same non-fiction category, as do sketch comedy shows, such as *Saturday Night Live*. Within the entertainment community, anything that is not a continuing character or stand-alone staged *vehicle*—or program—is considered to be non-fiction.

News certainly fits within this genre as well. However, despite my attempts to appeal to as wide a variety of employers and buyers as possible, I did not compete to produce news shows. Those who do news specialize in that genre and, while there is occasional crossover, it is rare.

Except for news producers, all non-fiction television producers are capable of swinging from format to format within the category. Whether the producer is producing an *Oprah*-type talk show or the latest in the series of meet-someone-and-fall-in-love-forever-in-six-weeks reality-show formats, the rules are the same. There are specific abilities, skills, objectives, and goals the responsible producer must have. From hiring the *talent*—the person or people on camera—to supervising the post-production, the role of producer is to make sure that the notion of "Let's put on a show" results in a polished finished product.

In the course of a single day as producer, I spoke with every member of my staff as well as advertisers, company executives, station representatives, etc. From the time I entered the studio until the time I left my office, I had more sensory input than an average person has in a month. Everything worked according to the clock because, based on our production schedule, at least two shows had to be "put to bed" by the end of the day. Never did a show go unfinished or over budget. It could not—not if I expected to be considered for another gig. Believe me, Hollywood is not a city in which there are secrets. If I did not deliver a show, all my competitors would know about it within minutes—and be lined up to compete for my position.

In this book I have covered every aspect of the career of non-fiction producer—from conceptualization to sale, from pilot to series, and all through the production of a series. No matter what your specific interest, and except for ever-improving technology, the rules you will need to follow as an aspiring producer in the non-fiction television genre will be reflected here. Whether you are a news producer who selects the headline story of the day and the order in which all stories will be broadcast, which may actually change on air because of breaking events, or the game show producer who must make sure that all five shows come in on time and on budget, the producer is the person in charge. The job is often thankless because perfection is expected, and the blame for any foul-up, no matter what the cause, is placed squarely on the shoulders of the producer.

My 3,000 episodes of national television gave me experiences and exposure to people that I will recall and recount for the rest of my life. Describing the many faces of a producer and the many kinds of producers, I have included some of my stories from the shows I wrote/produced/executive-produced, most of which were very successful. Unfortunately, except for my sitcoms such as *Welcome Back, Kotter* and *Three's Company,* none can be seen in reruns. I think of the wonderful interviews we did with actors such as Sir Laurence Olivier, Jack Lemmon, and other personalities who are no longer alive, and rue that the shows on which they appeared are stuck in a vault. Their words are part of television history. However, even though you may not know the particular shows or the figures that appeared on them, their stories and those of their producers remain universal. No matter what shows are being aired as you read this book, you can bet that the staffs have similar wonderful tales of people with vindictive personalities, weird habits, unusual idiosyncrasies, egomaniacal streaks, etc.

That said, whether you actually plan to become a television producer of non-fiction shows or are a student or are just curious about how it all comes together, I hope you will all benefit from and enjoy this book much as I did when I read a similar book five years before I began my career.

May this book inspire you to keep the flame burning for quality television through the years.

—Steve Clements

1
DEFINING THE TERM "PRODUCER"

HOW THIS CHAPTER FUNCTIONS

The question "What does a producer really do?" is certainly valid, one that should invite a short answer beginning with, "Oh, the producer is the person who..." Unfortunately, the answer is not that simple. First of all, there is not just one producer. Rather, there are *many* producers who serve many functions. Usual cocktail, quick-bite conversation does not allow for a detailed description of the many functions and types of producers, but this book is the forum in which I can finally give the proper and complete answer to "What does a producer really do?"

Within this chapter I shall describe each type of producer that exists in the non-fiction television world and the separate function each serves in order to explain why the different types of producer are necessary and what is similar in all the jobs. This includes the Show Runner, Line Producer, Producers of Individual Segments or Shows, Research Coordinator/Producer, Field Producers, Talent Bookers/Producers, Post-Production Supervisor/Producer, Head of Promotions/Producer, and finally the Executive Producer.

TYPES OF PRODUCERS

The Show Runner

First, there is the producer who takes command of the moment-to-moment and day-to-day details of the show. This includes hiring and supervising the staff, deciding what will and will not be included in each show—assuming it is a series. These duties include, in addition to coordinating the casting of each segment and each episode, making sure that the series is adhering to the budgetary allocations for each aspect of production that was approved at the outset, and creating a rhythmic flow of activities in conjunction with other producers, staff members, technical crews, post-production personnel, among many, to make sure every show is delivered for airing on time and on budget.

This producer is called the *show runner*. It doesn't matter what the actual title because that is negotiable. However, the best analogy is to compare the show runner to a baseball manager. While the baseball manager reports to a general manager as well as the team owner(s), the baseball manager is still perceived by the players, the public, and the journalists as the driving force behind the team. He is lauded if the team is successful, and fired if the team is losing. The same is true for the show runner.

Also, like a baseball manager, the show runner works with other producers, who, like the manager's coaching staff—the pitching coach, the first- and third-base coaches—are professionals and expert at what they do. In the case of producers, though, this list of personnel can also include those who occupy their roles in name only or hold their titles in lieu of salary increases or other sought-after promotions.

The Line Producer

Running a show is like running a household. You know what your take-home pay is and allocate a certain amount of money for rent, food, entertainment, etc. If you go over your budget one week, you must economize the following week. Similarly, every show has a budget that cannot exceed the amount of money being paid by the sponsors. Every possible expenditure has to be broken down into dozens of categories.

The *line producer* is in charge of creating and supervising this budget, and working with the show runner to make sure the show stays on budget. Together, they decide how to compensate for an over-budget category—whether they will sacrifice another category the same week or amortize the extra expense over several subsequent weeks. Typically, the line producer also takes care of other nuts-and-bolts tasks, such as supervising the crews, coordinating the submission of required paperwork from the network or studio, and working with the payroll department to approve expenditures by crews locally and in other cities.

The line producer absorbs a tremendous amount of information each week. Therefore, good communication between this person and the show runner is essential to avoid budget abuses, identify violators, and amend overages. My line producers always helped keep me in line by unhesitatingly informing me when my creative ideas were "too rich" for the production.

Producers of Individual Segments or Shows

The show runner supervises a staff of producers/*segment producers*, whose job it is to *pre-interview* guests. Pre-interviewing is speaking with guests, usually via telephone, to prepare them for the subject areas and questions that will be covered by the host or hosts. These producers help shape the guests' responses to appear as anecdotal as possible. Otherwise, many guests would give bland, one-word or one-sentence answers and seem to be avoiding a subject. This reflects poorly on the host and the show, and obviously encourages viewers to seek more exciting fare.

Consequently, these producers spend a great deal of time on the phone, engaging the potential guests in conversation to create more relaxed dynamics. The producer is listening for dramatic, funny, or other types of stories that will elicit the desired audience reaction. Once those stories have been identified, the producer's role is to instruct the guest to tell the story that will have the greatest impact when the interviewer asks a particular question. The producer then scripts the segment/show with notes that indicate what to expect from the interview.

At the studio or location the day of the show, this producer again reviews the questions and anecdotes with the guest. While on-air, if the guest forgets a particular story, the producer will hold up a reminder *cue card*. Therefore, when you see a question posed on shows such as *The Tonight Show with Jay Leno* or *Dr. Phil*, the host, show runner, and this producer already know what story to expect. Did you realize these discussions were *pre-set*—arranged in advance? They have to be. After all, producing a show means shaping it so that each moment is as informative and entertaining as possible.

In the past, these producers of segments or shows were known as segment producers. There were many magazine programs, such as *Today*, *Good Morning America*, and *Hour Magazine,* and one producer could be responsible for only one or more segments on the show. However, with the current trend toward one-subject television programs, such as *Oprah*, *Montel*, and *Jerry Springer,* the segment producer has become the person in charge of an entire episode. As a result, segment producers insisted on eliminating the word *segment* from their titles. Since then, the show runner has had to work with the producer of each show to make sure both have the same vision for each episode.

Research Coordinator/Producer

The research department of a major non-fiction show has several people collecting as much information as possible about guests and the subjects to be covered, as well as seeking out potential stories. While they may all be known as researchers, these titles are also negotiable. For instance, the head of the department may be known as the research coordinator or *coordinating producer* or *research producer*, while the rest of the research staff might be called *associate producers*. Titles and money are all a matter of leverage. Perhaps the production cannot pay as much as a researcher wants, but is willing to use the word *producer* in the person's title in exchange for this lower salary. In television, the operative word is *negotiation*.

Field Producers

While the segment producers/producers are responsible for the studio portions of the show, a show supported by enough money usually has a separate line item for *field producers*. Field producers travel around the country either to do separate on-the-road stories or to shoot specific footage to augment stories being produced in the studio. When there is a limited budget, part of the duty of the segment producer/producer is to do production/post-production on all footage shot outside the studio.

Talent Bookers/Producers

The talent booker has one of the most nerve-wracking positions, particularly when trying to get a commitment from the *star handlers*—the agents, press agents, managers of major stars, each of whom has dozens of requests for appearances by their celebrity. As a result, the chief talent booker is usually extremely well paid, especially if the person is capable of the *get*—securing the commitment of major stars or personalities who limit their schedule of appearances. As a result, the talent coordinator title is often upped to the title of *talent producer*. The lesser deities, those who are not so experienced or well connected, are given the *talent coordinator* titles. Can you imagine the pressure on the talent coordinator when a call comes an hour before taping that the major booking has canceled? The entire production team is alerted, and the talent coordinators make desperate phone calls to their closest allies among celebrities, publicists, and agents, promising limos, extra money—anything—so that the "hole" in the show about to tape will be filled. My method of dealing with these circumstances was to tape extra segments with celebrities, and, when possible, keep one interview on hold for such an emergency.

Post-Production Supervisor/Producer

If the budget of the show is low, the associate director can handle the supervision of the editing process. However, this is preferably done by a person who is coordinating all aspects of each show to ensure quality control. The person who supervises this process is called the post-production supervisor or, if negotiated well, the supervisor could be called the *post-production producer*. Can you imagine what it would be like if someone did not make sure that all editing notes were made so that the final product was exactly as intended?

The post-production supervisor takes all studio pieces, *field pieces,* which are produced outside the studio, unsynced voiceovers, and pick-ups and puts these elements in place so continuity is ensured in the completed show. I remember one incident when the host of a show appeared in one sports jacket and tie and, after going to a ten-second pre-taped "teaser," reappeared in a completely different outfit in the post-production tape. Often shows are not taped in sequence, and such problems are impossible to avoid, given the pressures of time. The post-production supervisor/producer catches these mistakes, discusses them with the show runner, and sees to it that the show is delivered devoid of such bloopers.

Head of Promotion/Producer

Every show has a promotion department that produces both television and radio *promos*—advertisements that promote the program. This department also devises campaigns for important ratings periods and coordinates personal appearances by the host(s) of the show. Because a truly creative promotion executive is hard to find, these individuals are often given a producer title such as *promotion producer* as part of the offer. The promotion producer typically supervises a staff to develop these promos.

Executive Producer

The *executive producer,* to go back to the baseball analogy, is the general manager equivalent. He does not usually become involved in every call or decision of every day. Instead, he works with the *front office*—the company executives—to determine their needs, wants, and what will make them happy at any particular moment. The executive producer also meets with the show's sales staff to discuss weaknesses, including possible cancellations, and how either to prevent them or to begin campaigning for other stations in the same *market*—city and/or region.

Finally, the executive producer is the person who looks at the big picture. When is it time to replace the set? Is the format becoming stale? Has the music started to sound as though it belongs to a past era? Is the subject mix becoming too predictable? Why have ratings started to erode? Is a small cosmetic change needed, or must there be a turn-over of staff, talent, or format, for instance?

The executive producer also makes himself available to speak to those who run the station *affiliates*—those stations that air the show. For example, if there were complaints about a particular segment, or ratings were low in a particular market, the executive producer might want to devote a segment a day for a week to that market. He might choose to coordinate a visit by the host of the show to a city in which renewal is in doubt. Generally, a visit by the host generates enough of a stir to make a difference. This effort often results in a ratings *spike*—a sudden, and usually temporary, surge in audience response—which serves to help the salesperson close the deal to air the show for the following season. Such a move would be initiated by a meeting between the show's promotion producer, show runner, and the executive producer.

In other instances—although difficult to believe—executive pro-ducers are figureheads who have nothing to do with any aspect of the show. They may have an executive producer title for any number of reasons: The person is the host/star of the show, the personal manager of the star, or a relative; a person who came up with the concept and was allowed to keep the title after giving up all responsibilities and most of the income promised; or an executive who had been discharged and for whom the title is part of the exit deal. The key motivators in Hollywood are perception and control. Sometimes there are four or five executive producers associated with a show. However, probably only one is an active participant in the show.

When the talent, host, or star becomes the executive producer, the whole scenario changes. I spent about six months as the show runner for an early morning show where the host was the executive producer. As a result, I had to be careful about the performance notes I gave to the talent because he was also my boss. I was being paid to make him the best he could be, but was in danger of insulting him and ran the risk of being fired as a result. In reality, the two of us got along well and, luckily, he liked my sense of humor and trusted my judgment.

However, he was also a bigot who expected me to follow his orders without fail. For instance, when hiring the staff, he told me without hesitation: "Stevie, I don't want no niggers, spics, or fags. You got me?" Yes, I could have resigned. But, if I were to resign each time I encountered prejudice in Hollywood, I would never have worked!

If you watch the logos at the end of shows such as the David Letterman-owned Worldwide Pants that produces David Letterman's show and Jay Leno's Mad Dog Video that produces *The Tonight Show with Jay Leno*, you have to realize these men hold the power. Yes, the network must be pleased with their performances, but their having all the power is something like not having separation between church and state. Sometimes decisions must be made in the best interests of the show, which may not benefit the host. But when the host does not realize his own strengths and weaknesses (which is often), the show runner must play to what the talent *perceives* to be his strengths and weaknesses. Perception and reality are not always the same, and any producer who displeases a star may be tossed out. The producer will then have a bad reputation about his inability to forge a positive relationship with *any* talent. It's a very delicate and uneasy balance.

A common misconception is that the head honcho, the guy calling the shots on any television show, is the executive producer. The image of the powerful executive producer, who makes all decisions, causes all employees to quake in their boots, hires and fires at will, and snaps his fingers so that his wishes will be immediately obeyed has probably been amplified by the appearances of executive producer Lorne Michaels on *Saturday Night Live*. In sketches he appears as himself, the benevolent but determined deity whose mandates must be carried out. In reality, he has made so much money for NBC for so many decades that he possesses more power than ninety-nine percent of executive producers in the non-fiction arena. Even with an executive producer as powerful as Michaels, though, *Standards and Practices*—the censors—have the real control. They study every line of every script for every show, including *Saturday Night Live,* to make sure that it fits within the current guidelines of the network.

While *Saturday Night Live* has certainly been successful in pushing the envelope, it is impossible for it or any production not to square off with the network censors occasionally. I have witnessed deal-making between the executive producer and Standards and Practices that was as ludicrous as it was hilarious. During the 1980s, words that are freely used these days, words such as *bitch, hell*, and *bastard*, had to be traded as though they were baseball cards. I remember howling when the executive producer of a made-for-television movie agreed to eliminate one *hell* for two *bastards*.

The funniest experiences that I endured with Standards and Practices were when I was at *Mickey Mouse Club*, which I executive-produced for The Disney Channel. Most people remember the show from the fifties when it was as an icon of wholesomeness, but thirty-five years later it needed to be more hip. As a result I spent more time on the phone with the elderly woman from Standards and Practices in Burbank than I did with any of my loved ones.

When my assistant would announce, "Paula is on the phone," I would groan and brace myself for a long "sex chat" with this woman in her seventies. Another big problem with Paula was that she had a hearing problem, which was being poorly corrected by two hearing aids obviously built by someone with a perverse sense of humor. Not only did Paula have problems with certain gyrations in dances, lyrics in songs, and what she considered to be innuendo in the scripts, but she also demanded to view entire episodes following their final edits. In other words, after a show was completely done, Paula would decide if it was done.

Once Paula viewed a perfectly innocuous musical number and wrote me one of the "much desired" pages of notes that typically preceded our lengthy chats. I couldn't believe my eyes! On one page, Paula wrote that during a particular *time code*—the exact moment wording appears on the work tape (19:22:30—19:22:45) she heard the words *f—* and *s—*. Of course I knew this was not true since I viewed every tape after each of several edits—and always viewed it after the final edit. Just to be sure, I asked for a copy of the tape, sat in front of a monitor, and listened with an ear to the speakers to those supposedly foul fifteen seconds—which, of course, weren't there! However, when I spoke with Paula at length, she insisted that those two words were inserted in an audio overlay. I treated her gently, arguing that it was not heard by me nor by the associate director or editors in the editing bay, which had the finest speakers available. At the same time I couldn't help but laugh silently as I listened to this Victorian woman using the offensive words with abandon. Since she would not be convinced otherwise, I told her that I would ask my two leading supervising executives at The Disney Channel as well as other top colleagues to listen to those "smutty" fifteen seconds. One by one, all of them went down on their knees, with their rear ends up and ears pointed to the speakers, as I cued the tape to the right section. None of them heard it. The incident, like many others, meant hours of work wasted on a figment of this woman's imagination.

I use this example to illustrate a basic point: The executive producer supervises the staff, has the major vision for each aspect of the production, and has approval and disapproval rights for anything. However, once the executive producer makes a decision, the studio or broadcast or cable network has the right to veto that decision. After all, each of them is paying for the production!

Then there are the individual stations that broadcast the program. If there is something aired that their viewers consider offensive, calls will flood the switchboard. The result is that the network and/or production company will be called and the executive producer is held responsible. If sponsors drop out, a station will often threaten to drop the show unless the ratings are outstanding. The executive producer would be held responsible here too.

Ratings

Ratings are the best guarantee for any executive producer's survival with a production. Complaints to any of the network/production company's clients usually put an executive producer's survival in doubt. This is why contracts have options for dismissal as soon as the negotiated deal will allow. This is so prevalent today that *networks*—the broadcasting entities such as NBC, CBS, ABC, and FOX—and production companies usually choose a thirteen-week option. This means that, even if an executive producer is fired during that thirteen-week period, the amount to pay him off will not be substantial—it can never exceed his pay for a thirteen-week period.

When there is a problem, the executive producer's first line of defense is to blame members of his staff, which usually satisfies the studio/network's need to find a scapegoat for a problem. Therefore, the first ratings shortcomings can be covered by promising changes in the direction of the show. And to change the direction of the show, the executive producer usually suggests firing key personnel and replacing them with those who will uphold the "new" vision—the one that will supposedly get the improved ratings.

The same holds true for questionable choices that he or even those prior to his arrival made. However, there reaches a point—usually quickly—when the executive producer can no longer hide from the axe. That is when his contract is settled, including the agreement about how the executive producer's exit from the show will be worded in the press release that goes to the trade publications. The usual reason given is that the executive producer feels his every personal goal has been accomplished and now wants to expand his horizons—that it was never his intention to remain with the program past the launch. The network/production company then expresses regret about this decision, wishes the executive producer well, and expresses thanks for the exceptional job that was done.

If the executive producer had the good fortune to have a guarantee of a year or so, and several months remain on the contract, it may be said that he is either remaining with the program as a consultant or developing new projects for the network/studio. Occasionally, it is the fired executive producer who negotiates such a statement. By having an office and a phone, he gives the illusion that he still has a job at the studio/network. This is a wonderful solution for everyone—the change is made, and the executive producer seems to have been promoted rather than fired.

There is just one problem. Hollywood is a very small community, and, no matter what the trade magazines say, everyone knows the truth within days. In fact, in many cases, the Hollywood community knows that an executive producer is to be fired *before* the executive producer knows. I was a player in one of these dramas. At the time Fred Tatashore, my former supervising producer of *Dinah!*, was executive producer for a Regis Philbin show for NBC. This was a show that ran before Regis began his current highly successful association with Kathie Lee and Kelly Ripa. Even though I was supervising producer of another show, I knew that Fred was going to be fired because NBC contacted me about taking over his job. However, I was told to keep it a secret because Fred didn't know.

Somehow Fred saw my name on the vice-president-of-daytime-programming-for-NBC's calendar. As he had been playing "the game" for several decades, Fred knew immediately what was to happen. He went to the vice-president of daytime programming and said, "Earl, if you're planning to replace me with Steve Clements, I quit." Earl said that quitting was fine, since he was going to be fired. I later met with the vice-president as well as with Regis and was offered the job. I turned it down for two reasons: one, I had a job on a new hit and wanted to enjoy the rare ride of a success, and two, I saw the poor ratings and realized the prognosis for the Regis Philbin show. In fact, a colleague who had just lost his job of twenty years as executive producer for Mike Douglas because of cancellation took the job amid much fanfare. The show was cancelled four weeks later.

WHAT ALL PRODUCERS SHOULD EXPECT

A Life-Consuming Job

As you can now see, titles do not necessarily tell the tale. As a matter of fact, I have seen even more new titles come about in recent years, titles such as senior executive producer. It's frightening to think that there is now someone above the executive producer when that individual is supposedly the "top gun."

It's like a child's matching game. Name the job and the title to see if they go together. In fact, if you are looking for a job in television, it would be a good idea to call the show production office to ask for the name of the show runner. That way, at least you will know you are getting to one of the key decision-makers. Oh, and don't make any assumptions from the credits on the screen. Every show has its own politics, so don't try to define a person by his or her title alone.

The reality is that there are many capable men and women in non-fiction television creating quality programming—and many people coming along for the mad ride. However, I wouldn't have given up one moment of producing the creative ride.

When I began producing, it became my life. Throughout my career I wore many hats. In addition to producing on-air shows, I created new shows, found talent, searched for financing, created viable budgets, envisioned each aspect of production, and supervised the artists in each category from sets to lighting to direction. And these are just a few of the roles that a producer/executive producer must play. By the end of the book you will have a more thorough understanding of the expansive nature of the role and why it can consume one's life.

That said, whether my title was producer, supervising producer, or executive producer, I never gave up the role of show runner, the role I found the most satisfying and fun. Satisfaction and fun were what drove me toward producing, and should be the motivating factors for anyone entering an industry in which success is elusive and always being challenged.

Producing must be about the joy of putting on a show. It is that basic. The thrill of conceiving a show or a particular episode of that show and supervising every detail of it from the initial idea to the viewing of the *final cut*—the last edit with all refinements that will become the air show or the program as it will be broadcast—is what must motivate you. For me, the constant threat that a show would not be taped and delivered on time was what made the job exciting. It was my equivalent of the thrill drivers get racing cars, when their lives are on the line every time they climb into the driver's cockpit. If you are a person who is easily thrown or is prone to becoming ill, this is definitely not a job you should consider. However, if you like constant—and I do mean constant—challenges, ones that need immediate resolution all day as well as the occasional middle-of-the-night ones, you will find no greater fun than being a show runner.

For me, no other job ever gave me the high I got each day as show runner for almost a quarter century. When I drove to work in the morning, I knew by the time I drove home, depending on the production demands of the particular show, between one and six new episodes would be completed except for editing.

It was so satisfying that, rather than give up the show runner position to a supervising producer when I became executive producer, I took on the duties of the executive producer while continuing with those of show runner. How? By putting a highly capable person in the job of supervising producer. That person was usually Margie Friedman, who had worked with me for so many years and so many thousands of shows that I could trust that her decisions would reflect my own. In a sense, it was a professional marriage. Margie knew what I liked, how I would react to segments, situations, personalities, and show elements. That gave me the freedom to perform the traditional roles of the executive producer, while making sure each moment of every show was one of which I approved.

In this book I have written about the production aspects from the perspective of show runner, and the creation and selling of new shows from the perspective of the executive producer. In future chapters, you will learn how a show is put together, the relationship among all the people responsible for a non-fiction show, and an approach to selling programs to networks, syndicators, and cable channels.

Whether you find yourself drawn to this stressful but exciting world or decide to forego it because life is too short, I hope you will enjoy your individual journey.

2
MAKING A SUCCESSFUL PILOT

I t is naive to think that the process of getting a show on the air is first to produce the best pilot possible, then to wait by the phone for the news that the series is a *go*—picked up for air. Nothing works that smoothly in television. The actual path has many bumps between pilot and series—*if* there is a series. It is important to understand that perhaps only ten percent of all pilots result in a *series order*—a decree from the studio or network for the executive producer to produce a designated number of episodes at a predetermined price. The other ninety percent or so go to a place I like to call Videotape Heaven.

I was fortunate that many of my pilots did become series. However, the path was never easy, direct, automatic, predictable, or unchanging, and it was always beset with severe twists and turns. To think it would be otherwise would be a pipe dream. While many of the pilots I produced became series, others were never seen and remain only in my personal library, months of effort and anxiety resulting in tremendous disappointment. I do have to admit some of the series were clunkers that still leave me wondering, "What was I thinking?"

PRODUCING A PILOT, TAKE ONE: *EVERYDAY*

I began my adventures in the world of creating non-fiction television pilots and series in 1978 when Group W Productions (Westinghouse) hired me as an associate producer on a new, and unnamed, show. This was after my experiences as a writer with *Welcome Back, Kotter, Three's Company,* and Dinah Shore's talk/variety series.

Once I was hired, I and the other producers desperately tried to create the perfect title for this new show we had been describing as "the marriage of *Saturday Night Live* and *Good Morning, America*"—talk about a strange coupling! We finally named the show *EveryDay* and turned our attention to casting and taping the pilot.

Casting and Taping the Pilot

The initial casting for *EveryDay* took place in New York City, where we spent several months interviewing actors for a comedy troupe that would be something like the one on *Saturday Night Live*. As the associate producer, I was told to look for a "Goldie Hawn," "John Travolta," and other prototypes for the ensemble. I knew the types of performers I wanted to find for our comedy troupe since I had directed my own comedy sketches in my nightclub days. However, the candidates that agents thought were appropriate and sent over to be interviewed amazed me: one "John Travolta" was five feet four inches tall, balding, and blatantly gay.

After even one day spent interviewing bubbly "Goldie Hawns," I was "perky-ed out" and happy to send the best of the group to Philadelphia for a weekend of intense auditions held in the studio that Mike Douglas used during the week. Nothing could have prepared me for that weekend of auditioning. It seemed more a week at a summer drama camp, complete with flirtations, romances, and out-and-out romps. It was like the television version of *A Chorus Line*—but only a fraction as good as the Broadway Pulitzer-prize winner.

Casting the troupe was nothing compared to the main problem—no one could figure out how to unify the comedy and information portions of the show. The two producers—former *Tonight Show* talent coordinators—decided to "snow" buyers by packing the show with celebrities rather than showing an actual show format. Therefore Chevy Chase, George Carlin, and Suzanne Somers—to name just a few—made appearances in the pilot.

The sixty-minute pilot took six and a half hours to record and was shot in Los Angeles at tremendous cost because everyone in the cast had to be transported to the West Coast. Just the amount of time it took to tape should have indicated that the show was not ready for production. During the taping, the "producers" stood at the back of the audience with their arms folded, acting like impresarios. I had learned from my season at *Dinah!* that to *floor produce*—to supervise the moment-to-moment happenings as the show is taped—the producer should be just feet from the hosts, talking to the talent between segments, throwing questions on *cue cards* to the talent, speaking with the control room during the action, and generally controlling every action in the production. So, when David Salzman asked me if I would floor produce on the fly, "because these guys are useless," I took over the production and completed the pilot, ragged though it was.

Turnover

Immediately after the production of the *EveryDay* pilot finished, "the impresarios" were fired. Because David Salzman had had enough faith in me to ask me to floor produce the show, I believed I was in an excellent position to be named producer of the series. I flew to New York to convince Salzman of my excellent candidacy, believing he would want to hire the person who could deliver the best show.

Instead, it turned out Salzman needed to hire a producer whose name would give the show "sizzle" in the marketplace since the pilot was awful but had been sold to enough stations to go on the air. Even when a specific producer is not the best fit for a show, industry custom is to seek a name who will raise eyebrows, get noticed, and receive publicity—in other words, change the karma of a show that seems to be in trouble. Salzman hired Viva Knight as the new producer. Knight had never produced a talk/variety show of the *EveryDay* type. Her claim to fame was that she had produced *Mary Hartman, Mary Hartman*, a late-night soap opera starring Louise Lasser. Because Knight had made *Mary Hartman* a hit, Salzman believed she could do the same with *EveryDay*. *EveryDay's* first ratings were dreadful, barely registering a blip on the radar screen.

Now came my lesson in the sudden appearance and disappearance of bodies in an attempt to convince station groups, advertisers, and Westinghouse executives above the television division that *something* was being done to ensure that a hit status was just moves away.

As is the case in many industries, no one is ever fired in television production. Instead, everyone "resigns in order to seek other and better opportunities." No mention is ever made in any of the trade papers about whether those opportunities ever did appear, but the spin is that, perhaps two to three weeks into the production of a new show, a key player, who is receiving a six-figure income, decides one day: "I don't know why, but I just think I want to leave a secure job to find a new opportunity."

I particularly remember the meetings held in the conference room to announce that a key member of the staff had "resigned." David Salzman would make these announcements and, as part of the exit deal, would extol the virtues of the now-departed employee, explaining how that individual had helped the show reach its current status. Everyone in the room would turn around to figure out who was missing.

One day we looked around and realized that David Salzman himself was missing! Someone from the Group W corporate office was giving David's speech—this time about David! The new producer, Carla Singer, and executive producer were introduced as the show's saviors, as though they actually had a vision of how to make this oil-and-water concept a breakthrough success. After much palaver, it was, "Let the games begin—again!"

I made sure that Carla Singer and I bonded so I could avoid being part of her purge, even though it appeared that my position was as secure as any position could be with a show with a miniscule viewing audience. I represented continuity in the show's production since I had been around since its inception.

Tweaking the Product

However, the problem of integrating the subject matter with the comedy material remained at the forefront, starting with the show's established format. Typically, a host would introduce a serious sub-ject. Then our troupe of "zanies" would put a light spin on the subject and, after gales of *sweetened* (laughter and applause added during post-production), we returned to the host and a guest expert to begin the interview of substance. In one seemingly apocryphal situation, we introduced an oncologist who was to give us the latest news about a particularly virulent form of cancer, which was followed by, "However, before we speak with the doctor, here is Murray Langston with a look at the lighter side of cancer." My toes did not uncurl for at least a week, and all the show's producers prepared résumés.

Nonetheless, we continued to take steps to increase the show's vis-ibility. One action I took in youthful desperation demonstrates how a producer's assertiveness sometimes results in poor judgment. The then mayor of Cleveland was to appear on our show. He was so unpopular and so disliked that our production office received a death threat for him a few hours before the taping. Of course, we alerted the proper authorities to take responsible measures. However, I decided in order to make the nation aware of this show—at which we had worked so hard and yet had no recognition factor—I would alert the newspapers and television stations about the death threat. I told them when and where we were taping, and encouraged them to send representatives. When his honor entered the stage, no one would go within twenty feet of him. I stood at the side perusing the audience for possible assassins—but mostly for journalists. My ploy for media attention had worked, but at what cost?

Despite our best efforts and a nearly hundred percent turnover of staff, we were again called to another of those meetings. This time we were meeting the new president of Group W Productions, Bill Baker, who had been named to replace David Salzman. Baker's claim to fame was that he had once produced the local *Cleveland Morning Exchange*, a background that seemed to lack the necessary depth for his new position. We had already heard stories about him, such as his refusing to take medication before having dental surgery in case he had to take a phone call. In my book—which this is—that is lunacy! Baker's official introduction to the staff and cast was no surprise. He welcomed us all, told us how glad he was to be there, congratulated us on our efforts, and told us *EveryDay* was being cancelled.

A chill went through my body when I learned that I was on the verge of unemployment yet again. After eight more shows—making a grand total of 103—*EveryDay* would be history—or worse, a trivia question! In a classic "Hollywood moment," the female host of the show, Stephanie Edwards, worried out loud about having just purchased an expensive home in Santa Monica. Without missing a beat, Baker asked her how many bedrooms the house had since he was in the market for a three-bedroom house in Los Angeles.

The pall of producing eight essentially extraneous shows was relieved to some extent by "gallows humor." One particularly mordant wit created a puzzle in which you had to match former employees of the show with the positions they once held. Since I was one of the few originals who made it from start to finish, I was the official winner. My prize—unemployment.

TAKE TWO: *AT NIGHT*

Ready for a new challenge, I found myself answering a phone call from Jim Devaney, an NBC salesman who fancied himself an entrepreneur. He had left NBC's sales department to find work as an executive producer in television. Devaney knew absolutely nothing about television production, but, as a salesman, had contacts to various sources of money. He obtained money for a pilot and asked Joel Tator, who had created Tom Snyder's *Tomorrow* show in the early 1970s, and me to come up with a late-night show for "Sweet Dick" Whittington—a then-popular radio personality in Los Angeles.

The idea we conceived was very much in keeping with the experimental, "push the envelope" style of the era, just a few years after the premiere of *Saturday Night Live.* Our *At Night* would be a fantasy-fulfilled type of show in which a middle-aged man—Whittington—had the opportunity to participate in Walter Mitty-style experiences in exotic late-night locations all around the world. We would place him in bizarre experiences, such as a séance in the home of a deceased celebrity, a ceremony at a witches' coven, and at a then-chic sex orgy palace called Plato's Retreat. It was television conceived to convince the viewer to stay up late, particularly on Saturday nights, when we hoped it would be shown.

Joel and I agreed that our budget limited us from shooting all of the show in the field. Since an international flavor was something we could not afford, we taped all segments in Los Angeles, San Francisco, and Las Vegas. I wrote, Joel directed, and we co-produced. The staff consisted of Joel and me. Jim Devaney popped in occasionally to find out how to make television. As stated earlier, the title executive producer does not mean the person with the title has any experience or knowledge. In this case, Jim's title merely meant that he had the funds to produce the show.

Our segments for the pilot included a nude audition for a sex film in an office on Hollywood Boulevard, in which several young ladies literally removed their clothing, which we carefully shot, for an actual sleazy producer who was making a real-life movie. Joel and I could not believe our eyes and barely contained our laughter when Whittington stripped naked for his own audition. In another segment, we went backstage to the famed female impersonator club, Finocchio's, in San Francisco, and watched as men became women. As part of that segment, we asked excited Japanese men as they got off a tour bus what they were expecting to see that night. One of the men replied, "I'm expecting a very young time."

In Las Vegas, one of the hotels gave us access to the "Eye in the Sky," where men actually stood watch above the blackjack tables to see if anyone was cheating. Can you imagine how technological advances have altered that system of security?

All our segments were done "tongue in cheek," and we presented a well-produced, well-edited pilot—one that was perfect for late Saturday night. Unfortunately, in an all-too-common scenario, Devaney ran out of money before figuring out how to market the program as a series. Joel and I walked away with a well-done show with no future.

TAKE THREE: *THE DAVID LETTERMAN SHOW* —ALMOST

Walking away from *At Night* and taking charge, for the first of what would become many times, of my television career, I made an appointment with Chuck Gerber, the head of late night for the NBC *O&O*

stations—owned and operated by a network, as opposed to a station that simply has a contract to run the network's programming.

As Chuck watched the *At Night* pilot, he laughed and covered his eyes at all the appropriate places. Flipping out the cassette, he shook his head and told me that he "could not believe it." I questioned him: "What can't you believe?"

"I can't believe that we just gave Rollins-Joffe [managers of the hottest comedians in show business at the time, including Billy Crystal and Robin Williams] $20,000 to develop this concept for David Letterman." Letterman was a virtual unknown at the time. His name had been heard only at The Comedy Store in Los Angeles and as a featured player on a flop Mary Tyler Moore variety show. "They're just thinking about it; but you already have it on tape, and we want this show to replace *Rock Concert* on Saturday nights following *Saturday Night Live.* I'm going to set up a meeting for you to meet with Letterman."

This was fine with me, not because of Letterman, but because the executive from NBC wanted to place the show in the schedule exactly where it belonged—on Saturday night at 1:00 A.M. Also, what could be better than to follow *Saturday Night Live,* which even in 1978 was already becoming a legend? Further, the contract with Dick Whittington had been loose enough to allow us to replace him without any charge to the production. Basically he had no claim to the series whatsoever. Tator and I would only have to buy out Devaney since he had investment money in the pilot.

I met David Letterman at Universal Studios, where Rollins-Joffe had their offices. It was pouring that day in Los Angeles, a rarity in a city that averages ten days of rain a year. Letterman seemed very shy— the type of shy that makes the other person feel uncomfortable. It was hard to start a conversation, although he was pleasant and seemed eager to see the show. Without umbrellas, we both dashed to a screening room, laughing at how we were getting drenched to the bone. Once there, I placed the cassette into the machine, and enjoyed listening to his appreciative laughs. I knew if he liked the show, the time spot was ours, so I watched the tape while listening nervously for Letterman to laugh. At the end of the screening, Letterman shook my hand and said, "You have a very funny show. I like it a lot." We then ran through the rain again and waved good-bye.

The waiting period after an incident like this is nerve-wracking, painful, hopeful, and exhilarating—not to mention self-critical whenever you begin to feel too exhilarated or hopeful. I knew anything could happen. Finally, after about a week, I spoke with Larry Brezner from the Rollins-Joffe office, who told me that the company decided to *pass* on —turn down—the project. I asked why since David had seemed to like it so much. "Oh, Dave liked it, but we don't feel there's any money in late night! We're going to make a deal with NBC for a daytime show." That line still remains with me after twenty-five years. David not only flopped terribly with the daytime show, but went on to become one of the most successful late-night hosts in history. His latest deal with CBS became a battle for his services between that network and ABC, which resulted in his receiving an annual salary of more than $33 million.

I have included this story not to relive one of the many "almosts" we all endure that might have changed the course of our lives, but also to underscore the nature of the producer's life after pilots—quirky, unpredictable, with heights of optimism followed by depths of despair. It is a roller-coaster ride, one that becomes part of everyday existence when television producing is your life.

TAKE FOUR: *GOOD AFTERNOON*

During *EveryDay*'s last week of production, I got a reprieve of sorts when Carla Singer called me into her office to tell me there might be a job for me after all. Group W was launching a massive research effort to determine why *EveryDay* had failed (I could have told them in two words—*it sucked*) and wanted to use the findings to create a new show. She wanted me to work with her on the new show. In other words, Carla and I were to be the only two left standing after the cleansing. Without written confirmation of this new job, however, I packed up my desk and went out to the parking lot after the last taping just like everyone else.

Two months and millions of dollars later, Group W's research indicated that daytime female audiences did not like a female host—in this case, Stephanie—to dominate her male co-host. The male co-host, John

Bennett Perry, is perhaps now best known as the father of Matthew Perry, Chandler Bing on *Friends.* Women, Group W found, wanted a host to be a "husband substitute," one who would provide information they could use.

When Carla called me two months after the last episode of *EveryDay* aired, she asked me to take the nondescript title of "development executive" during what the initial stages of what was now known as *Good Afternoon* and help her find that husband substitute. While no one could answer my query of, "What happens if the show is scheduled in the morning?" I understood that I would later be named producer to her executive producer of the pilot and series.

During the next few months I contacted agents for every "has-been" male television and film star in his forties—someone with name recognition and few to no job prospects who would be grateful for an opportunity to host a new show. Our prototype in 1979 was David Hartman, who had gone from actor to host of *Good Morning, America.* Among those we interviewed were Robert Reed (*The Brady Bunch*), John Gavin (*Imitation of Life*), and Gary Collins (*The Sixth Sense* and other TV series). Reed was an incredible egotist and self-proclaimed intellectual who refused to understand we were creating a program for an audience of women who were home during the day. I scripted a show for him that was appropriate for the genre we were producing. However, despite his being warned not to intellectualize in a way more appropriate for PBS, he opened his test show by quoting the architect and philosopher Buckminster Fuller. Hopeless! John Gavin, on the other hand, seemed to be missing movable parts. He was a nice man, but his body language said aging Ken of Ken and Barbie fame. I felt that no one would have been able to warm to him. I championed Gary Collins who, despite his lack of training, had the potential, warmth, and good looks to be the perfect husband substitute.

Then I got another of the shocks or life lessons that are all too common to the Hollywood experience. I knew that Carla had been flying to New York recently but never questioned why. It turned out she had been interviewing potential producers for *Good Afternoon.* The result of the interview process shocked me: She had hired a man named Marty Berman to be the show's producer. When I protested, referring to our previous arrangement, she said she had promised to *try* her best to make me the producer. Instead, she said I was to become the senior associate producer. I was absolutely devastated. Would my next promotion make me *super senior associate producer?*

To try to ease the strain of the situation, Carla set up a meeting between Marty Berman and me—a mutually uncomfortable and singularly disastrous breakfast. Marty knew I had expected to become the show's producer, and I knew Marty saw me as "disposable." No one wants an angry "wannabe" looking over his shoulder. To illustrate the fact that I was disposable, Marty flexed his muscles during the host auditions by jumping onstage, walking in front of me, and making it known that he was my superior, even though I had been working with the hosts until that point.

I also found his style objectionable. For example, when Robert Reed was stiff, he called him to the side, smacked him on the butt, and yelled, "Hey, Bob, relax!" That sure did the trick!

TAKE FIVE: *HOUR MAGAZINE*

Despite changes in the hierarchy, I was allowed to hire Gary Collins as the host. Even though he was an actor who had never hosted a television show, he had the "husband-substitute" image we were seeking for our target audience of women at home, and the name recognition from starring in four prime-time series.

Just as we were about to begin production on the new pilot for the show, Bill Baker, who had been named president of Group W Productions after David Salzman, was fired—I guess he no longer needed that three-bedroom house. He was replaced by Edwin T. Vane. Vane, who always shook hands as though he were running for president and never made solid eye contact, had spent nearly thirty years in programming at both NBC and ABC. He made it instantly clear he would have liked to cancel production on this show. Women, he said, had no interest in this sort of "blather." They wanted entertainment. However, instead of canceling the pilot, Vane began making changes in front of and behind the camera. First, he insisted the show be called *Afternoon Magazine* since the company already had a show called *P.M. Magazine*. *Afternoon Magazine* was designed for syndication, which meant each station could air it at any time. Therefore, if the show were aired in the morning, the name would be odd to say the least!

Vane also decided to hedge his bets by hiring Dick Clark, who wanted to do the show, as the host of a second pilot. Finally, because he preferred to work with men, Vane relegated Carla to developing new shows—before she left to take a development position at CBS. Marty and I continued working on what was now to be known as *Hour Magazine* in a partnership that was to last eight years. Marty was appointed executive producer—and I was appointed producer! Marty and I had gotten over our differences.

TAKE SIX: SUCCESS!

To finalize the decision between Gary Collins and Dick Clark as the two possible hosts, I shot two pilots on two successive evenings. The staff was the same; the set was the same; even the co-host, Pat Mitchell, was the same. However, we shot different field segments with each of the two men, making sure neither was given an unfair advantage.

Since talk/magazine series reflect the nature and personality of the host, each of these tapings was completely different. Collins was a neophyte as a host. I gave him a short course on media training and stood just out of camera range to help him in any way that I could. He was charming but stiff.

Dick Clark was…Dick Clark. Need I say more? Dick Clark has been the same Dick Clark since the mid-1950s, whether on *American Bandstand, Bloopers,* or at Times Square on New Year's Eve. His persona is imprinted on every television viewer of nearly any age. Since I had never worked with him before, but had watched him since I was a child, it was a fascinating experience. Several hours before the taping, I observed him standing alone onstage practicing every line, every chuckle, and every "seeming" ad-lib. I was astonished. I had expected him to coast into performance mode at will.

Just before the taping, he was introduced to an admiring audience and gave them the patented Dick Clark charm. When it came time to introduce his co-host, he was unrestrained in his praise of her—she was a top professional, one of the finest with whom he had ever worked in all his years in television. Then all at once he gestured for me to come over. I was only a few feet away since I was floor producing and curious about what he wanted as I hurried over to this Mt. Rushmore of television hosts. Putting the portable microphone behind his back, Clark whispered in my ear, "What's her name?" Instead of blurting out, "How could you forget the name of a woman you just canonized?" I just whispered back, "Pat Mitchell."

Without missing a beat, he introduced her as though he had interrupted his introduction to ask a production question. As Clark chatted with his "friend" Pat, we began taping. Clark said every word of every line exactly as he had practiced it a few hours earlier. Every chuckle was emitted in exactly the same cadence at exactly the same place, and every gesture was an exact duplication of the one he had rehearsed. It was an amazing revelation to me as someone who had grown up studying the classic hosts of television.

After the pilots were completed, everyone at Group W Productions believed that the crowning of Dick Clark as host was a given. We had a round table meeting with all the key executives and even the creative consultant.

The creative consultant on a pilot typically has little or no role, but receives a huge salary because this makes the chief executive appear to be properly cautious about the creative aspects of the show. The individual in that role on this pilot was a lovely man with an outstanding background as the director of variety shows during the 1960s. However, he was elderly, and had absolutely no background in talk/ magazine television. But, when he began to speak, we all leaned in. "I've been watching *The Today Show* and *Good Morning, America*, and thinking to myself, What makes the difference between an average segment and something wonderful? and it suddenly came to me," he said. We all leaned farther forward as though he were dispensing the wisdom of Obi Wan Kanobi in *Star Wars*.

"The secret is that...every segment must be...compelling!" Wow! Heavy, dude! Our jaws dropped at this revelation. The realities of an executive meeting in television can often be more ludicrous than any satire written about the industry.

At this particular round table meeting, I was the only one who felt that Gary Collins was the appropriate choice. He was the right age, was handsome, and brought a fresh, appealing personality to the scene. However, he would need to be trained. Although everyone disparaged my opinion, it was standard to conduct *focus groups*—videotaped sessions with a target audience, in this case women, who express their feelings about a product or a program—to choose the host. A company was hired to run the focus groups, and I attended several sessions in San Diego. I was delighted to find my instincts were correct. While everyone liked Dick Clark, there were no surprises with him. The women said they would not tune in because they already knew what his show would be like. Instead, they wanted to know more about "the young blond guy," Gary Collins. He was, they felt, handsome and gentle, and they would like to spend time with him each day.

Gary Collins won the job, and Dick Clark returned to his regular job of being Dick Clark everywhere else. The only problem was that Gary did not know how to do the job. Which is why I spent a year with him going from city to city and station to station as he hosted and I produced local morning shows while the regular hosts were on vacation. Each afternoon, after working with the local staffs in Philadelphia, Boston, and San Francisco, Gary and I would sit down for several hours to view the playback of that morning's show. We discussed technique, and he quickly improved.

As Gary became more confident, he had more fun and, as a result, I had dozens of wonderful hours of him on tape from which to edit a pilot presentation for *NATPE*—National Association of Television Program Executives. Station executives gather each January at NATPE to see what new shows will be available in syndication for the following year. At this time, salespeople try to get commitments from stations to buy a show. In 1980, when Gary entered the NATPE convention, everyone wondered how he could compete with the hot names at that time, names that included Toni Tennille, Bert Convy, and John Davidson. Gary and his wife, former Miss America Mary Ann Mobley, as well as Marty Berman and I, worked the *Hour Magazine* suite in San Francisco for ten hours a day, five days straight, never accepting a negative response from a station buyer. We were not the salespeople, but we could chat with the buyers and build up excitement and enthusiasm for the show.

It was like the final quarter of the Super Bowl with excitement running high. After station buyers were primed to sign, we turned them over to the "official" salespeople. After every signing, an announcement was made about the percentage of the country that had been sold. The goal was seventy percent. That number is significant because national minutes can only be sold to advertisers when at least seventy percent of the country is covered. A syndicated show makes its money from two sources: the *license fee*—the agreed-upon weekly amount that the station agrees to pay the distributor for the right to air the program—and the *national minutes*. There are twelve minutes of advertising in each hour—three are usually sold by the distributor on the national level at high prices that create profits, while the local station sells the other nine minutes. In recent years the distributor of "monster" hits such as *Wheel of Fortune, Jeopardy!,* and *Oprah* is allowed to demand a more even split of the minutes.

By the end of the convention, *Hour Magazine* was the talk of the industry. We had outsold every competing program and were announced as a "firm go" for the fall of 1980. It was a long and hard-won victory—a high in my life that I will never forget.

My road from pilot to series for *Hour Magazine* was a long one, but one for which there was a happy ending—six Emmy nominations, two Gold Awards from the New York International Film and Television Festivals, three Media Access Awards for the work we did in the portrayal of the disabled on television, as well as awards from the American Bar Association and the American Medical Association, and an eight-year run.

TAKE SEVEN: A COUPLE CAUTIONARY TALES

Success is wonderful. Remember, however, the entire television industry is a gamble, and the lure of money, even initial money, is often enough of an impetus to take a measured—okay, not always measured enough—risk.

In the 1990s, eighteen years after the *At Night* experience, I became involved in a pilot in which I received the initial one-third payment for expenses upfront. The second third was to come during the production period and the final third upon delivery of the finished tape. However, after casting and beginning pre-production of this program, *Living Well,*

I got word from my *executive in charge of production*—the person whose job it is to make sure that the show is budgeted correctly and that monies spent do not exceed monies received—that the second payment had not been received on time. I continued as though nothing were wrong, but did call the distributor, who assured me that it was just a matter of liquidity, and that the next check would arrive within a day or two.

I then did something I had never done before, never did again, and strongly advise you never to do ever. Some of the props had to be picked up with a U-Haul, and since we had so little money, I gave the production assistant my personal American Express card to rent the U-Haul. The driver of the U-Haul immediately slammed it into a power pole while backing out of a driveway. The pole fell on another car, and nearly killed the people inside. Who would have been responsible? Me! Luckily, the *E&O Insurance* (Errors & Omissions, insurance that protects the policy holder from damages due to most mistakes of negligence), a policy that is essential for any production, picked up the tab, which was far greater than what I made from the pilot.

The second check finally did arrive from the owner of the company, who I learned was a cocaine addict with such tremendous debts that he was about to be arrested for grand larceny. I was not a happy man! Nevertheless, we taped the show and it went well.

Unfortunately, the company fell apart shortly after the taping. Thankfully, the final installment of the pilot costs did arrive before the president of the company was arrested. I decided not to market the tape myself because at this time the "blood and guts" television of *Jerry Springer* and other Springer wannabes was dominating the market. Our tasteful health and wellness show was what is called *soft*—I hate that word. Soft means that a show has no *edge*. Edge is supposedly young and hip, but I wanted no part of hip as exemplified by Springer and the other atrocities. It was about this time I began to question whether or not I belonged in a field that pandered to the lowest common denominator in any audience.

During this same general period, I sold a *run-thru* of a concept about which I felt very strongly. A run-thru is often a "cheapie" presentation, meant to put the concept "on its feet" so that the buyers can determine if they want to spend "bigger bucks" on an actual pilot. It can also be used in place of a pilot. A run-thru can take the form of a non-taped stage presentation, or a "home video" done with no scenery.

This run-thru was a show on dispute settlement through mediation rather than litigation—an alternative for most of us who can't afford the fees charged by attorneys. Lorimar-Telepictures, the company that had bought the concept, did not pick up the run-thru, so it was once again my property. I began to sell it myself to other distributors along with a new host named Bill Lincoln, an intelligent, charming man and a giant in the field of mediation. I flew him down from Seattle to meet with potential buyers. After all, a charming host can seal a deal, and Lincoln had a Bostonian accent that made him sound like John F. Kennedy!

We were meeting with the top executives at Universal Studios when Lincoln casually mentioned a trip he had taken after recovering from his third heart attack. I nearly had my first! I could see faces drop. Of course, Universal did not buy the show; buyers do not want to invest millions of dollars in a host who might drop dead on them. The only other interested company was Worldvision, which was owned by Aaron Spelling. I went to Seattle with Spelling executives, who watched Lincoln at work and were delighted. However, just as they were about to agree to the program, *Dispute Center*, another legal-personality show, appeared on the scene. Worldvision decided to put its money on her instead—Judge Judy! I can't say that I blame them, but this was yet another example of an "almost" that could have changed the course of my life.

3
SELLING THE SHOW

YOU'VE GOT A PILOT, NOW WHAT?

If you find yourself a bit confused about who the seller is, who the buyer is, what the marketplace is, and into which category the producer or executive producer fits, it is perfectly understandable. That's because nearly everyone is both buying and selling in order to reach the goal of getting a show or shows on the air.

THE SELLING CHART/HIERARCHY

Playing the game of getting a show on the air is like playing a board game in which the winner is the first to reach the "end zone." In fact, to make it easier to understand this race to the end, I have created a flow chart. At first glance, it may look like an unsolvable Chinese puzzle, which in reality is not far from the truth. However, the chart does lay out the levels of the "food chain," some of which can be bypassed, in order to "win." Please follow along as I explain the meaning of the multiple highways and byways on the chart.

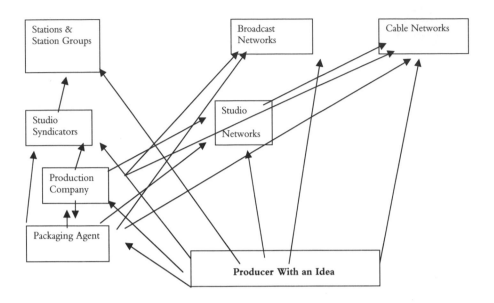

At the bottom of the chart is the "Producer With an Idea." If your first impression is that his job looks like the one that David had in slaying Goliath, you're beginning to understand the scope of the task ahead. Let's say you are that producer. As the lines indicate, you can choose any number of directions in which to begin your quest. You must understand, though, that at any point you may tumble back to the bottom, and may even morph into "Producer *Without* an Idea."

Initially you can bring your *show concept* (a show that is fully developed on paper), *notion* (an idea that needs money for development), signed talent, or edited video presentation to a packaging agent, the syndication arm of a studio, or the network arm of a studio. Sometimes these are the same executives. Or you can go directly for the "score" to a broadcast network, a cable network, or the individual stations and station groups that air syndicated shows. Each route is "shark-infested," and some will definitely send you spinning back to Start.

Broadcast Networks, Cable Networks, and Stations/Station Groups

Before you begin your game, let's make sure that you understand what each of those three "winning" boxes at the top really means. We'll start with the boxes in the center and on the right, because their definitions are less confusing

Broadcast Networks

The broadcast networks are NBC, CBS, ABC, Fox, UPN, and the WB...that's easy. If any of them decide to put your show on the air, you have won the game. This is not, however, the way the game is usually played and won.

Cable Networks

At the right are cable networks, which continue to proliferate as digital television replaces analog. Lifetime, USA Network, Nickelodeon, ESPN, and HGTV are just a few of the cable networks. These cable stations differ from broadcast networks in that they are *narrowcasts,* meaning that they are targeted to a particular segment of the population. However, like the broadcast networks, cable networks can decide to put your project on the air, which is not likely unless you are well known, have an outstanding track record, or are a production company that has done business throughout the industry.

Stations and Station Groups

The most complicated box to understand is the one at the left, Stations and Station Groups. The general managers of these individual stations and the executives in charge of the station groups, such as Sinclair, Post-Newsweek, Belo, etc., have stations in cities all over the country. Let's say that the executive at the Sinclair stations loves the tape of the talent you have signed and decides he would like to put the show on the air next season. If that station group owns stations in twenty-three percent of the country, you don't have enough *coverage*—percentage of the country that will air the show, with seventy percent as the minimum—to announce a launch. You do, however, have tremendous leverage to go to the *Studio Syndicators*. These are the organizations that sell programs to individual stations and station groups.

These studio syndicators include Paramount and King World, both owned by Viacom, which also owns CBS and UPN, and has its own station group; Fox, with its own station group; Buena Vista, which is part of the Walt Disney Company, owns ABC, and has its own station group; NBC Productions, owned by NBC, with, of course, a station group; and

Warner Bros. Domestic Television, a part of AOL TimeWarner, which has a station group through the WB Network. In other words, these syndicators own everything and are selling to stations and station groups within their own company as well as externally.

One difference between a network and syndication is that the network can make a final decision to put a show on the air, while syndicated shows must sell to many stations and station group owners in order to get the *green light*—go-ahead for production. A syndicated product makes its money from two basic sources: the license fee paid by each station for the right to air the episode and the national minutes, which is the time sold to national advertisers, whose commercials have already been inserted into the episode. National advertisers will not participate unless seventy percent of the country has been *cleared*—sold for air.

Syndicating a show seems to be less desirable than having a firm commitment from a network because syndicating takes more people, more effort, and more time—usually about a year—before the entire process is complete. However, the advantage that has always worked in my favor is that, just as it takes more than one entity to put the show on the air, it also takes more than one entity to take it off the air. For example, if a syndicated show tanks in Pittsburgh but thrives in Boston, the producer could shop the show to other stations in Pittsburgh. If no station wants it, it can still remain on the air as long as the ratings are strong enough to warrant renewal in at least seventy percent of the country. I strongly believe that my career in television lasted as long as it did because of the rules of syndication. They allowed a marginal show the time it needed to demonstrate its strength, whereas a network would have quickly *pulled it*—taken it off the air.

The First Step

Now that you know about the three giants at the top of the flow chart, let's return to the various routes that a producer can take to secure a "win."

The Agency
One path takes the producer to an agency, such as William Morris, CAA, or ICM, as well as to smaller, boutique agencies. If you are a client

of one of these major agencies, it would behoove you to utilize their services. Of course, they would be serving their own interests rather than yours since any deal they made with a studio or network would require that they receive approximately five percent of the weekly budget and eight percent of the profits. This could be likened to selling your soul to the devil. However, if that same agency decides to support your project, it may have the necessary clout to open the right doors.

The Production Company

An agency can also introduce your project to a production company, one with one or more successful products on the air. More often than not, the production company the agency selects will be one it represents. Like everything else in television, this has both its pros and cons. The positive side is the production company, because of its proven successes, will be more welcome at a network or studio than you as an independent producer would be. The negative side: Because the agency is representing both you and the production company, your participation both creatively and financially might be at risk. To whom will the agency have more loyalty, the production company bringing them "big bucks" or you with a wonderful idea but no cash?

You know the answer! I know of at least one producer who lost millions of dollars because he trusted his agency. Alan Sacks, who created the 1970's hit sitcom *Welcome Back, Kotter*—the story of a Brooklyn boy who returns to teach at the high school from which he graduated—brought the idea for the show to The Komack Company, also known for *Chico and the Man* with Freddie Prinze. The owner of the company, Jimmie Komack, loved the idea for *Kotter* and suggested that Sacks sign with his agent, the William Morris Agency. Sacks was thrilled that he would actually be represented by the world's most-renowned agency. Although William Morris welcomed him with open arms, the deal they made for Sacks deprived him of any of the benefits of Kotter's smash-hit status. Sacks did produce the initial season of the show, as promised in his contract, but was fired once it was completed, despite its success. He has never received any royalties for the past quarter century; in fact, he never earned another cent from the show after that first season—and never again had a show that was as successful as *Kotter*. Consider this path in the game to be dangerous.

By the way, my first job as a freelance writer in Hollywood was with *Welcome Back, Kotter,* for which I contributed scripts for two seasons. I convinced the producers to grant me entry to this show because, like Kotter, I had also returned to teach at the Brooklyn high school from which I had graduated.

The Packaging Agent

Look back at the flow chart at the beginning of this chapter. See the arrows going between the production company and the packaging agent? I relayed the Alan Sacks story to warn you to keep your eyes open and bring an entertainment attorney into all negotiations. Nevertheless, any drawbacks can be overcome by being properly cautious, so if you as Producer With an Idea have an opportunity to sign with an agency or a production company that has "heat," do so. It is an excellent way to strengthen the possibility of selling your project to one of the top-row biggies.

The Second Step

The next level on the road to getting a show on the air is listed as Studio Syndicators and Studio Network. With the consolidation of executives at some studios, this group may be the same. In fact, you and the production company and/or agency should consider any or all venues for your project and listen to what each group of executives says is best for your project. However, at this point, the levels to the top begin to blur.

Studio Syndicators

Let's say, for example, you, or you and your team, bring a project to Disney. You believe it would be best for your project to be syndicated through Disney's Buena Vista division, but Disney feels it is a network project, and, therefore, targets it for ABC, which it also owns. Or Buena Vista feels that the project is not for broadcast, but would be perfect for cable.

Because Disney owns ABC, Lifetime, ESPN, A&E, The Disney Channel, ABC Family, and several other cable networks, it is the broadcast network, the cable network, and a tremendous station group all in one. Despite this, synergy among the divisions is not necessarily harmonious. If Buena Vista decides to syndicate the show, it must convince the ABC O&Os that its decision is a good one. However, the Disney O&Os don't constitute seventy percent of the country. Therefore, Buena Vista needs the support of the *affiliates*—those stations that it doesn't own, but that run its programming. Neither the O&Os nor the affiliates are required to support the shows that Buena Vista proposes. If they don't agree, they may reject the project. Or, because of the tremendous capital in the Disney organization, the project may be tested on one or more of its stations. If it fails, it loses money. If the test is successful, it will likely win the support of both the O&Os and the affiliates. This is one tremendous advantage of dealing with a studio with huge resources.

Studio Network

Nevertheless, it is likely that, without station support, Buena Vista might pass on the project, but still recommend it for one of Disney's cable networks. However, if the relationship between Buena Vista and a cable executive is acrimonious, you might have to begin again at square one. Further, you might have to tread carefully, since the knowledge that the project has been rejected by one division might prejudice the executives in another division.

The fact that the television industry has been consolidated to just five or six major studios—AOL TimeWarner, Disney, Fox, Viacom, General Electric—has made the playing field for producers much smaller. It was more fun when I began to sell television programs because I had more than a dozen "stops" or "times at bat." All I needed was to have one of the dozen studios like my idea, and the project would be *put into development*—signed for the purpose of leading to a pilot.

However, despite the drawbacks presented by fewer studios, there has been a huge increase in the number of venues in which a program can be placed. In 1976, there were three television networks and syndication—that was it. Now there are six television networks, syndication, and nearly one hundred cable networks. So find a project and run with it.

One more note: It seems as though the producer at the bottom of the flow chart is lowly and all alone. Nothing could be further from the truth. In reality, if the producer has any track record at all, he will receive dozens of calls weekly from producers with fewer credits and shows to sell. The buying and selling goes both ways and never ends.

History of Network Syndication

When television first began in the late 1940s, there were two networks: NBC and CBS. In 1953, a third network, ABC, began its programming and, for years, those were the only three choices a viewer had for original programming on the national level. By the late 1950s, syndication, in which original programming was sold to individual stations or station groups, emerged.

One of the tremendous advantages of syndication is that the fate of the program is not in the hands of just one decision-maker. For example, if NBC wants to cancel a program, it simply notifies the production company and/or studio that it is cancelled, and the program becomes history. Not true with syndication. Let's say you are producing a program that airs on WNBC in New York, and WNBC decides not to renew your show for the following season. Instead of closing up shop, working through syndication, the company distributing the show now has the opportunity to speak with each of the competing stations in the market.

It is for this reason that I chose syndication as the primary venue for the programs I created. In syndication, you can be a powerhouse in Philadelphia and a complete fiasco in Seattle. If the station in Seattle cancels your show, the sales executives gather statistics about ratings and demographics in the more successful markets in order to convince a competing station in Seattle that the show's failure in that city was an anomaly. Demographics are a profile of the makeup of the show's audience, with age being the most important factor. The younger the demographic, the more money advertisers are willing to spend for a thirty-second commercial. Ideal viewers for advertisers are between eighteen and forty-nine, with eighteen to thirty-four considered the most desirable range. Supposedly, people in this demographic are more likely to change their brands of toothpaste than those over thirty-five.

When selling to a new station in the same city, sales executives will try to demonstrate that the original promotional campaign was not strong enough or that the show was in the wrong time slot in order to convince a general manager to give the show a chance. Often the company that distributes the show will even pledge money for the proper promotion of the show.

Whatever the arrangement, this has proved very beneficial for some shows, equating to multi-decade runs enjoyed by *Oprah, Wheel of Fortune,* and *Jeopardy!.*

By the late 1970s, cable stations began to surface, beginning with the pay channels HBO and Showtime. These channels had the advantage of being subscriber-supported and, as a result, were not subject to the same censorship rules and concerns. After all, there were no sponsors. Their only concern was *churning*, which means that a subscriber may cancel the service. When many people begin to churn, it means that the programming must be reexamined. Soon these basic cable stations grew to ninety-nine and all were developing original programming. All of these stations were on *analog systems* and, eventually, they grew to hundreds of stations on *digital systems.* The technical difference between analog and digital is that analog consists of continuously varying electronic waves that are transmitted depending on frequency; digital signals contain a sequence of voltage pulses transmitted over a wire medium. In short, with digital systems there are more channels to which programming can be sold. About this time, Fox, a fourth network, also appeared, followed shortly by the WB and UPN.

When I began creating programs for television, I had approximately sixteen potential buyers for every idea I had. Now, as mentioned above, there are only five or six companies that buy programming. This consolidation has hurt producers because the power of ownership is in the hands of these few giant companies. They finance the shows, control the content, air them on their network or cable outlets, and often even own the cable system on which it will be played. With power so consolidated in the hands of few, the independent producer must tread carefully.

A Word to the Wise

Before pitching a show or shows, register the concepts with the Writers Guild of America to protect yourself from theft. Make sure an attorney or agent knows that a particular show was pitched, to whom, and on what date. In other words, while it may be difficult for David to slay Goliath, everything must be done to maximize the safety of your possession of this intellectual property even before anyone hears the pitch.

But keep pitching, because perhaps just one show will result in at least a base hit, if not a double, a triple, or even a home run.

The Pitch

Every producer has different theories about how to pitch a project and just what, if anything, should be left to the discretion of the executive(s) taking the pitch. My technique changed, depending on whether or not I had the attention of the executive. If he were busy accepting phone calls and didn't seem to be paying attention, I would pitch as an "opener" a show I knew wouldn't be bought. By the time I received regrets about why that particular show would not work, I knew that I had his attention. Then I pitched the show that I *really* wanted to sell. It was almost as though the first show were an opening act, a throwaway.

Some executives will not tolerate more than one pitch per visit. In that case, I would try to get the executive's attention through conversation and not pitch my show until I had him laughing, attentive, and receptive. In case that project did not receive the reception I had hoped, I usually had one more project with me to try if I truly believed that the executive might be receptive to another idea. I might approach it by finessing the executive with a line such as, "I have one more project that I saved for last. But if you've heard enough, I'll save it for another time. However, if you don't mind hearing one more . . ." The executive then has the opportunity to decide. If the first project was viable, but not exactly what he wanted, another pitch may be encouraged.

That said, under no circumstance should a producer go with a "laundry list" of show ideas. If the executive cuts you off, not only will you sell nothing that day, but also any further meetings will be in jeopardy. In other words, the secretary will be informed that you are never to be on the list for meetings.

The Leave-Behind

The next rule is always go with a *leave behind*—a written treatment of the shows that were pitched. There are two reasons: First, if the executive hasn't decided whether or not to buy the show, he may read the treatment and like it better on paper and seal the deal. Secondly, the executive whom you pitched might have to pitch it at a meeting, in which case your treatment will become his "crib sheet." Therefore, make sure that everything you want said in that meeting is on the leave behind. State it as concisely and with vivid words and images. Without the leave behind, you must trust that the executive will be as effective as you were at selling the show at the meeting. That is unlikely! Those pages are crucial...they are the conduits to the sale.

The Leave-Behind Sell

When trying to sell a show, the obvious question a producer must address is, "How much will it cost per week?" While a producer may "ballpark" the figure and create a budget if or when the network or production company is ready to buy, the inclusion of a budget as part of the leave-behind demonstrates you are thinking both creatively and practically.

As a result, I have addressed the leave-behind as two separate entities. The first is the written pitch; the second is the budget for the show. The show I am using for demonstration purposes is a pilot that I sold to NBC called *Daytime*. I pitched this as an alternative to the glut of one-topic talk shows, which merely reprocessed the same subject matter, usually something to do with dysfunctional families. I felt that there was a need for a program that offered a combination of informational programming—such as I had produced for daytime audiences for years—along with celebrity interviews and musical and comedy performances. These had not been on the daytime scene since the demise of *Mike Douglas, Dinah!*, and *Merv Griffin*. I wanted the return of the band instead of canned music, and an hour that both entertained and left daytime viewers with the feeling that they had learned something—in other words, an hour well spent. This was important because focus-group participants expressed a sense of guilt if they watched a program that was just entertainment but could justify watching a program that also contained useful information.

The proposed program was to be hosted by a then relative unknown, Bob Goen (who later became co-host of *Entertainment Tonight*) and Dana Fleming, who had demonstrated popularity during her years as co-host of *Home*, a daytime show for ABC.

Please take note of the points I emphasize in the written copy for my leave-behind:

- Intelligent, appealing personalities with chemistry
- Informality
- Relationship between the two hosts as good friends
- Loose format
- Return of variety to daytime television
- Recurrent experts
- Visualization of a sample episode
- Fun factor
- Capable staff
- Contemporary and warm look
- The ability to create a sense of family for viewers

As you will see on the following pages, the leave-behind is a key element to the success of developing a new show.

DAYTIME

Starring

Bob Goen   **Dana Fleming**

Steve Clements Productions

1

DAYTIME

STARRING

BOB GOEN & DANA FLEMING

Television definitely does not need another host grilling bizarre guests about such boringly redundant life styles as "Menopausal Nymphomaniac Nurses." It's time to "return to the roots"--intelligent, appealing personalities with chemistry, who deliver an informal, entertaining program. Gone should be the strait jacket of the seven minute segment that stops abruptly when the time cue is reached. Gone should be the rigidity that dictates that the host should say good-bye just when the "good stuff" is just beginning.

DAYTIME , STARRING BOB GOEN & DANA FLEMING is a casual entertainment program, hosted by two proven daytime favorites. Bob Goen is a handsome, witty host whose many game shows, including WHEEL OF FORTUNE, gave him just a sliver of an opportunity to demonstrate his warmth and humor. Dana Fleming is deliciously deceptive in that her Kansas roots belie her naughtily appealing sense of humor. In addition, she projects her genuine honesty and caring about people. It is widely known that when she left HOME, the ratings dropped immediately by over fifty per cent. Also, when Bob and Dana co-hosted HOME, there was spontaneous combustion on screen.

The look of DAYTIME combines the nineties with the traditional. Yes, there should be a small band with a likable third person to play off. Yes, there should be a studio audience, demos, celebrities, and relevant information for a mostly female audience. There are various conversation and demo looks, as well as a band area, and a performance section.

2

However, emphasis must be placed on Bob and Dana's relationship as good friends. Most likely, they will spend time together at the top of the show sharing a story. However, if a first guest would be best at the top of the show to get us off to a good start, that's fine also. No rules! The show should find recurring guests who can always be counted upon for fun. These guests should not be "Dr. Joyce Brothers" rehashes from every talk show since Steve Allen. Instead, we should look for "characters" who are experts, as well as actors on TV series who would make for outstanding regulars. No one should appear every Monday or Tuesday, etc. The show will be watched for Bob and Dana. The booking of celebrities will be stressed, and there will be performances. In addition, if a guest is "on a roll" on a particular day, we apologize to the people who did not appear, and announce that they will return tomorrow (or not). As we said--up with fun, off with the strait jacket.

DAYTIME should not appear to be "produced." It's time spent with people we like, and, as a result, helps us to get through the day with a better attitude.

3

SHOW DETAILS

After writing that DAYTIME is a show without a "strait jacket", we certainly don't want to give details that stray from that concept. Rather, we want to elaborate about the "feel" and flow of the program on a daily basis.

Since this is a program that is driven by the personalities of the hosts as well as by celebrities, we feel that there should be at least two celebrities per broadcast. Because we are looking for celebrities to recur, one of the celebrities might be a frequent guest. In addition, there should be at least one performance during each show. This might consist of a song, a stand up comedy routine, a dance, or the type of unique performance we used to watch on the ED SULLIVAN SHOW. The difference is that no one will ever be booked for the performance alone. This is a personality talk show, and the performer must be able to work well with Bob and Dana. Therefore, whether a guest is a magician, a hypnotist, a contortionist, a circus performer, etc., his/her ability to have "fun" with Bob and Dana will determine whether the booking is done.

In addition, each day there must be at least one demo, with a limit of how many times a week we return to the same subject. Among the demos will be fashion, hair, cooking, make-up, and new products. Those specialists who add to the Bob/Dana chemistry will recur more often than the "big name" specialists who give us marquee value, but also a seven minute snooze.

At least one section of the program will be reserved for guests with one of a plethora of functions. We might have an author with advice about relationships, etc. It is important to note that these authors should have topics that are skewed to our

4

predominantly female audience, and should be selected because of his/her ability to elicit "juicy" information about Bob and Dana that our viewers will want to hear.

Besides authors, we will have experts (many recurring), who give us the information our target group wants to hear. New medical information based on Thursday announcements in the NEW ENGLAND JOURNAL OF MEDICINE is of particular interest. Although we do not want to promise or commit to specific experts, it is interesting to note that Dr. Dean Edell recently signed a deal with KNBC. His high visibility in the media, combined with his youth, bedside manner, easy going personality, and good looks would make him an outstanding prototype.for DAYTIME.

One segment of the show could also be an "oddball", in the tradition of TONIGHT or the retired TOMORROW show. Whether that guest is someone who dined last night with Elvis, was transported to Mars for its annual fall festival, or can speak twenty-six animal languages, it is most important that this guest give Bob and Dana the opportunity to crack jokes, laugh with each other without making fun of the guest, and, most importantly, give them someone to play off. The right "Hollywood gossip" will provide good, funny shock value, because Bob and Dana are just not part of the "in" scene (a major concept of this program). Bob returns to his wife in the valley after the program, and, of course, Dana's constant journeys back to her home town of Wichita does not allow her to have a "Hollywood lifestyle" (not that she would want it). Like most people, however, they are closet readers of the NATIONAL ENQUIRER at the super market (HINT: Choose the longest line, so that you can get through the entire issue).

In the course of an hour program there will be seven segments. With just a few exceptions, the first segment will be devoted to the "chat" between Bob and Dana.

5

Although they adore each other as friends, both are married, and Dana has two

children. We are to believe that this segment is the only time they have to share what

is going on in their lives. Two of the segments are celebrities, with at least one

performance (Total of three). One segment is a demo (Total of four). Another

segment is devoted to an author or expert (Total of five). An oddball, person in the

news, inspirational guest fills another segment (Total of six). The good-byes, thank

yous, and credits are in Segment number seven.

Do the guests leave after their segment, do they stay throughout the show, or do

they stay for part of the show is the question that is always asked about any talk show.

The answer is all of the above. WHATEVER WORKS for a particular show is how

the show runs down. Remember, no strait jacket! The only rule is to provide the

best, most entertaining show possible. Another question is "Are Bob and Dana

together in every segment, do they alternate segments, or does one do more segments

than the other? The answer to that question is also all of the above. Again, whatever

works for a particular show! In this case, however, there will be an emphasis on the

two of them working together, because it is their unique chemistry that will appeal to

the audience. Their relationship should reach the point that even the unspoken speaks

for itself. Whether they disagree with each other, are angry with each other, are

touched by a particular revelation, or are hurt by a remark, we know what they're

feeling. After all, we care about them, and watch them every day.

The people who surround Bob and Dana are key to the program's success. When

searching for recurring celebrities, the "fun factor" is essential. For instance, Park

Overall of EMPTY NEST is recognizable, outrageous, and, definitely, likable. We

must also make sure that these "special people" have durability. We don't want to find

6

out that we have run dry after three appearances. Constant testing should tell us whether our viewers want to see them more, less, or never again.

When it comes to staffing the program, we must combine people who have a wonderful background of working with celebrities, with those who have been honored for their work in the reality field. EVERYONE must have a sense of humor, and be part of the show family. We would encourage familiarity with the names and life situations of staff members, and they should be prepared at any moment to take their place next to Bob and Dana. Luckily, we know the right people for the available positions, and they are most willing to join us.

The look of the show should be contemporary and warm, as opposed to the prison cell look of most of the single subject "confrontation" shows. There should be a home base, a demo area, a kitchen, a performance area, and a band area. We are not trying to make the audience believe, however, that this is anything but a television studio, and, therefore, bumpers can definitely utilize the SATURDAY NIGHT LIVE kind of look in which we see the entire studio in motion. We might see Dana chatting with a member of the audience, or Bob walking over to the guest who is doing the upcoming demo, while the property master is setting the props. It's all a matter of feeling that you, the viewers, are part of the experience.

It is our hope that DAYTIME becomes identified with NBC in the same way TODAY, TONIGHT, LATE NIGHT, SATURDAY NIGHT LIVE, and LATER have given the network viewers a sense of belonging.

The Leave-Behind Budget

When NBC expressed interest in *Daytime,* they wanted to know what the weekly cost would be for doing a series. I was able to shortcut a number of steps by including the weekly budget in the leave-behind. Between the time that interest was expressed and the week it might take to prepare a budget, NBC could have cooled on the show. Therefore, with the budget already approved—always with modifications—they gave the green light to move to a run-thru.

By the end of the twentieth century, the difference between a pilot and a run-thru was negligible. In actuality, it was merely a matter of the executive producer's making little or no money and producing the demonstration show with a used set, smaller staff, and shorter preparation time—but the expectation for the onscreen result was exactly the same.

The budget you are about to examine was approved if the show had gone to series. The run-thru was a tremendous success—it was produced as a run-thru for about $80,000 but *looked* like a quarter-of-a-million-dollar pilot! NBC loved it and was about to put it on the schedule. In fact, as previously mentioned, it *was* on the schedule until someone at NBC decided that a medical show with Dr. Dean Edell could be done less expensively, and, as a result, *Daytime* did not receive a *pick-up*—in this case, *pick-up* means selecting the show to go on the air.

As you read the weekly budget of $251,621, look at the first page, which summarizes each cost. Toward the bottom, the budget differentiates between *above-the-line* and *below-the-line* costs. Above the line are the costs of the hosts, producers, researchers and materials, director, special guests, talent bookers, bandleader and musicians, and travel. Below the line are the costs of such production staff as the stage managers, associate director, script supervisor, production assistants, and accountants, in addition to the stagehands, audience coordination, set dressing (and/or props), wardrobe, makeup and hair, lighting, video, sound, music clearance, post-production, insurance, tape stock, etc. The third category is *total fringes*. These are the costs for such things as payroll taxes and Workman's Compensation. The total of the above the line, below the line, and fringes equals the total weekly budget for the show.

As you read the budget, you will learn the approximate salary for each person who participates in a non-fiction show. In addition, you will get a better idea of the number of people who are necessary to produce a show of the size described in the leave-behind. You should also begin to understand all of the expenditures necessary to deliver a quality daily program.

The Budget

You would think that, at a time when there are a greater number of channels being developed, there would be a greater number of opportunities for producers to create programs. However, while the number of channels has increased, the number of viewers has decreased. People have found other forms of entertainment, including the Internet. As a result, a smaller universe of people are watching many more stations, thereby giving each network or channel a smaller audience. Smaller audiences mean fewer advertising dollars, which translates to smaller budgets for shows.

I was fortunate to have had the opportunity to produce a tremendous variety of pilots and series with a variety of budgets. For example, one show was budgeted at $11,000 per episode, a figure that included talent, production facility, production staff, and the technical crew. This meant that I had to wear more hats than usual and was restricted to hiring only three staff people. I also had to cram the taping of six episodes into a single day to amortize the cost of the facility at which we were taping. It was an early-morning venture, and the advertising revenue was greatly reduced since most people were asleep at that hour. On the other end of the spectrum was a show I produced for $200,000 per episode. It had music, sketches, videos, and *reality segments*, and its five daily episodes cost $1 million per week. In order to produce that show, I had a staff of more than 150 people. Between these two extremes were programs with reasonable budgets.

Therefore, I made sure before doing my *pitches*—the meetings at which I offered my programs for sale—that I had at least a general idea of the budget constraints. Still, I was sometimes shocked when a studio or network agreed to do a pilot and/or series, and gave me a bottom-line price that left the quality of the show in doubt. Luckily, I could usually solve the problem with creativity and the suggestions of the talented group of people who traveled with me from show to show.

BUDGET
5 Shows
2 Tape Days

DAYTIME WITH BOB GOEN & DANA FLEMING
5 SHOWS-VIDEOTAPED OVER 2 DAYS
Revision #2
Budget Date: 10/11/91

Acct #	Description	Page #			Total
101	STORY,RIGHTS,CONTINUITY	1			3,775
102	PRODUCERS UNIT	1			17,627
103	DIRECTION	1			5,826
104	CAST	2			75,149
105	SEGMENT PRODUCER UNIT	3			6,198
	TOTAL ABOVE-THE-LINE	3			108,575
110	PRODUCTION STAFF	3			9,543
114	SET CONSTRUCTION	4			500
115	SET OPERATIONS	4			13,391
117	SET DRESSING	5			4,324
118	PROPERTY	6			3,488
119	WARDROBE	6			5,455
120	MAKEUP & HAIRDRESSING	6			3,784
121	ELECTRICAL/LIGHTING	7			12,344
122	PRODUCTION VIDEO	7			21,670
123	PRODUCTION SOUND	8			5,006
124	TAPE STOCK	9			4,577
125	TRANSPORTATION	9			1,335
131	STUDIO/STAGE RENTALS	10			6,000
	TOTAL PRODUCTION	10			91,417
134	MUSIC	10			5,000
135	POST PRODUCTION VIDEO	10			11,375
136	POST PRODUCTION SOUND	10			225
137	OPEN/CLOSE/BUMPER TITLES	11			800
138	PURCHASE OF VISUALS	11			2,000
	TOTAL POST PRODUCTION	11			19,400
143	GENERAL EXPENSES	11			5,580
144	INSURANCE	12			1,250
145	MISCELLANEOUS	12			25,400
	TOTAL OTHER	12			32,230
	TOTAL ABOVE-THE-LINE				108,575
	TOTAL BELOW-THE-LINE				143,047
	ABOVE & BELOW-THE-LINE				251,621
	TOTAL FRINGES				21,675
	GRAND TOTAL				251,621

Pg. 1

DAYTIME WITH BOB GOEN & DANA FLEMING
5 SHOWS-VIDEOTAPED OVER 2 DAYS
Revision #2
Budget Date: 10/11/91

Acct #	Description	Amount	Units	X	Rate	Subtotal	Total
101	STORY,RIGHTS,CONTINUITY						
101-02	RESEARCH						
	HEAD	1	WEEK		1,000	1,000	
	ASSISTANTS	1	WEEK	3	600	1,800	
	PAYROLL TAX	13.85	%		2,800	388	
	WORKMAN'S COMP	3.10	%		2,800	87	3,275
101-90	RESEARCH MATERIALS						
	SERIES	1	WEEK		500	500	500
					Total for 101		3,775
102	PRODUCERS UNIT						
102-01	EXECUTIVE PRODUCER						
	SERIES	1	WEEK		10,000	10,000	
	WORKMAN'S COMP	3.10	%		10,000	310	10,310
102-02	PRODUCER						
	SERIES	1	WEEK		3,500	3,500	
	PAYROLL TAX	13.85	%		3,500	485	
	WORKMAN'S COMP	3.10	%		3,500	109	4,094
102-05	ASSOCIATE PRODUCER						
	SERIES	1	WEEK		2,500	2,500	
	PAYROLL TAX	13.85	%		2,500	346	
	WORKMAN'S COMP	3.10	%		2,500	78	2,924
102-99	MISCELLANEOUS EXPENSES						
	SERIES	1	WEEK		300	300	300
					Total for 102		17,627
103	DIRECTION						
103-01	DIRECTOR						
	SERIES	1	WEEK		4,500	4,500	
	PAYROLL TAX	13.85	%		4,500	623	
	WORKMAN'S COMP	3.10	%		4,500	140	
	DGA FULL DIR	12.50	%		4,500	563	5,826
					Total for 103		5,826

GOOD COMPANY   Pg. 2

Acct #	Description	Amount	Units	X	Rate	Subtotal	Total
104	CAST						
104-01	HOSTS						
	BOB GOEN-SERIES	1	WEEK		15,000	15,000	
	DANA FLEMING-SERIES	1	WEEK		15,000	15,000	
	WORKMAN'S COMP	3.10	%		30,000	930	
	AFTRA	10.50	%		30,000	3,150	34,080
104-02	SPECIAL GUESTS						
	SERIES-5 GUESTS PER DAY	5	DAYS	5	569	14,225	
	SERIES-MUSIC GROUPS-3 WK	3	DAYS	5	281	4,215	
	PAYROLL TAX	13.85	%		18,440	2,554	
	WORKMAN'S COMP	3.10	%		18,440	572	
	AFTRA	10.50	%		18,440	1,936	23,502
104-09	TALENT BOOKER						
	SERIES	1	WEEK		1,200	1,200	
	PAYROLL TAX	13.85	%		1,200	166	
	WORKMAN'S COMP	3.10	%		1,200	37	1,403
104-10	TALENT COORDINATOR						
	SERIES	1	WEEK		600	600	
	PAYROLL TAX	13.85	%		600	83	
	WORKMAN'S COMP	3.10	%		600	19	702
104-21	BAND LEADER						
	SERIES-TAPED-30 HR RATE		ALLOW		1,732	1,732	
	PAYROLL TAX	13.85	%		1,732	240	
	WORKMAN'S COMP	3.10	%		1,732	54	
	AFM	9	%		1,732	156	
	AFM HEALTH/CRTGE	2.50	%		1,732	43	2,225
104-22	BAND MEMBERS						
	SERIES-TAPED-30 HR WEEK		ALLOW	3	866	2,598	
	PAYROLL TAX	13.85	%		2,598	360	
	WORKMAN'S COMP	3.10	%		2,598	81	
	AFM	9	%		2,598	234	
	AFM HEALTH/CRTGE	2.50	%		2,598	65	3,338
104-23	GUEST TRAVEL						
	SERIES-AIR	1	WEEK	4	1,200	4,800	
	HOTEL	2	NIGHT	4	150	1,200	
	PER DIEM	2	DAYS	4	50	400	
	GROUND	3	ALLOW	4	75	900	7,300
104-24	HOST TRAVEL						
	AIRFARE-HOSTS-SERIES		ALLOW	2	800	1,600	
	GROUND-SERIES	2	ALLOW	2	75	300	1,900
104-99	MISC CAST/GUEST EXPENSE						
	SERIES	1	WEEK		700	700	

GOOD COMPANY   Pg. 3

Acct #	Description	Amount	Units	X	Rate	Subtotal	Total
104	CAST (Cont'd)						
104-99	MISC CAST/GUEST EXPENSE (Cont'd)						700
						Total for 104	75,149
105	SEGMENT PRODUCER UNIT						
105-01	SEGMENT PRODUCERS						
	SERIES	1	WEEK	3	1,100	3,300	
	SENIOR SEGMENT PRODUCER	1	WEEK		2,000	2,000	
	PAYROLL TAX	13.85	%		5,300	734	
	WORKMAN'S COMP	3.10	%		5,300	164	6,198
						Total for 105	6,198
	TOTAL ABOVE-THE-LINE						108,575
110	PRODUCTION STAFF						
110-02	STAGE MANAGERS						
	SERIES-TAPE	2	DAYS		387	774	
	SERIES-TAPE	2	DAYS		387	774	
	PRODUCTION FEE		ALLOW	2	29	58	
	PAYROLL TAX	13.85	%		1,606	222	
	WORKMAN'S COMP	3.10	%		1,606	50	
	DGA OTHER	20.219	%		1,606	325	2,203
110-04	ASSOCIATE DIRECTOR						
	SERIES-TAPE	3	DAYS		417	1,251	
	SERIES-TAPE		ALLOW		29	29	
	PAYROLL TAX	13.85	%		1,280	177	
	WORKMAN'S COMP	3.10	%		1,280	40	
	DGA OTHER	20.219	%		1,280	259	1,756
110-10	SCRIPT SUPERVISOR						
	SERIES	1	WEEK		1,100	1,100	
	PAYROLL TAX	13.85	%		1,100	152	
	WORKMAN'S COMP	3.10	%		1,100	34	1,286
110-11	PRODUCTION COORDINATOR						
	SERIES	1	WEEK		650	650	
	PAYROLL TAX	13.85	%		650	90	
	WORKMAN'S COMP	3.10	%		650	20	760
110-12	SECRETARIES & TYPISTS						
	SERIES	1	WEEK	2	450	900	
	RECEPTIONIST-SERIES	1	WEEK		325	325	
	PAYROLL TAX	13.85	%		1,225	170	

GOOD COMPANY   Pg. 4

Acct #	Description	Amount	Units	X	Rate	Subtotal	Total
115	SET OPERATIONS (Cont'd)						
							1,402
115-21	AUDIENCE COORDINATION (Cont'd)						
	SERIES-TAPE		ALLOW	2	850	1,700	
	BUSSES	2	DAYS	6	350	4,200	
	PAGES-SERIES-TAPE	20	HOURS	4	15	1,200	
	PAYROLL TAX	13.85	%		1,200	166	
	WORKMAN'S COMP	3.10	%		1,200	37	7,303
115-22	AUDIENCE WARM-UP						
	SERIES-TAPE	2	DAYS	2	300	1,200	
	PAYROLL TAX	13.85	%		1,200	166	
	WORKMAN'S COMP	3.10	%		1,200	37	
	AFTRA	10.50	%		1,200	126	1,529
					Total for 115		13,391
117	SET DRESSING						
117-01	ART DIRECTOR						
	SERIES	1	WEEK		1,700	1,700	
	PAYROLL TAX	13.85	%		1,700	235	
	WORKMAN'S COMP	3.10	%		1,700	53	1,988
117-02	SET DECORATOR						
	SERIES	1	WEEK		800	800	
	PAYROLL TAX	13.85	%		800	111	
	WORKMAN'S COMP	3.10	%		800	25	936
117-16	PURCHASES/RENTALS						
	SERIES	1	WEEK		1,000	1,000	1,000
117-40	FLOWERS & GREENS						
	SERIES	1	WEEK		300	300	300
117-48	LOSS & DAMAGE						
	SERIES	1	WEEK		100	100	100
					Total for 117		4,324

GOOD COMPANY   Pg. 5

Acct #	Description	Amount	Units	X	Rate	Subtotal	Total
115	SET OPERATIONS (Cont'd)						
							1,402
115-21	AUDIENCE COORDINATION (Cont'd)						
	SERIES-TAPE		ALLOW	2	850	1,700	
	BUSSES	2	DAYS	6	350	4,200	
	PAGES-SERIES-TAPE	20	HOURS	4	15	1,200	
	PAYROLL TAX	13.85	%		1,200	166	
	WORKMAN'S COMP	3.10	%		1,200	37	7,303
115-22	AUDIENCE WARM-UP						
	SERIES-TAPE	2	DAYS	2	300	1,200	
	PAYROLL TAX	13.85	%		1,200	166	
	WORKMAN'S COMP	3.10	%		1,200	37	
	AFTRA	10.50	%		1,200	126	1,529
					Total for 115		13,391
117	SET DRESSING						
117-01	ART DIRECTOR						
	SERIES	1	WEEK		1,700	1,700	
	PAYROLL TAX	13.85	%		1,700	235	
	WORKMAN'S COMP	3.10	%		1,700	53	1,988
117-02	SET DECORATOR						
	SERIES	1	WEEK		800	800	
	PAYROLL TAX	13.85	%		800	111	
	WORKMAN'S COMP	3.10	%		800	25	936
117-16	PURCHASES/RENTALS						
	SERIES	1	WEEK		1,000	1,000	1,000
117-40	FLOWERS & GREENS						
	SERIES	1	WEEK		300	300	300
117-48	LOSS & DAMAGE						
	SERIES	1	WEEK		100	100	100
					Total for 117		4,324

GOOD COMPANY   Pg. 6

Acct #	Description	Amount	Units	X	Rate	Subtotal	Total
118	PROPERTY						
118-01	PROPERTY MASTER						
	SERIES	1	WEEK		1,100	1,100	
	ASST-SERIES	1	WEEK		600	600	
	PAYROLL TAX	13.85	%		1,700	235	
	WORKMAN'S COMP	3.10	%		1,700	53	1,988
118-16	PURCHASES/RENTALS						
	SERIES	1	WEEK		1,500	1,500	1,500
					Total for 118		3,488
119	WARDROBE						
119-02	WARDROBE SUPERVISOR						
	SERIES	1	WEEK		1,500	1,500	
	PAYROLL TAX	13.85	%		1,500	208	
	WORKMAN'S COMP	3.10	%		1,500	47	1,755
119-03	WARDROBE ASSISTANTS						
	SERIES	1	WEEK		600	600	600
119-16	PURCHASES						
	SERIES	1	WEEK	2	1,500	3,000	3,000
119-46	CLEANING & DYING						
	SERIES	1	WEEK		100	100	100
					Total for 119		5,455
120	MAKEUP & HAIRDRESSING						
120-01	MAKEUP/HAIR ARTIST						
	SERIES-HOSTS-TAPED	2	DAYS	2	350	1,400	
	SPECIAL GUESTS-TAPED	2	DAYS	2	400	1,600	
	PAYROLL TAX	13.85	%		3,000	416	
	WORKMAN'S COMP	3.10	%		3,000	93	3,509
120-16	PURCHASES						
	SERIES	1	WEEK		75	75	75
120-78	BOX RENTALS						
	SERIES-TAPED	2	DAYS	2	50	200	200
					Total for 120		3,784

GOOD COMPANY   Pg. 7

Acct #	Description	Amount	Units	X	Rate	Subtotal	Total
121	ELECTRICAL/LIGHTING						
121-02	LIGHTING DIRECTOR						
	SERIES-TAPED	2	DAYS		600	1,200	
	PAYROLL TAX	13.85	%		1,200	166	
	WORKMAN'S COMP	3.10	%		1,200	37	1,403
121-03	GAFFER						
	SERIES-TAPED	2	DAYS		350	700	
	PAYROLL TAX	13.85	%		700	97	
	WORKMAN'S COMP	3.10	%		700	22	819
121-05	LIGHTING BOARD OPERATOR						
	SERIES-TAPED	2	DAYS		300	600	
	PAYROLL TAX	13.85	%		600	83	
	WORKMAN'S COMP	3.10	%		600	19	702
121-06	ELECTRICIANS						
	SERIES-TAPED	2	DAYS	2	250	1,000	
	PAYROLL TAX	13.85	%		1,000	139	
	WORKMAN'S COMP	3.10	%		1,000	31	1,170
121-17	EQUIPMENT RENTAL						
	SERIES-TAPED	1	WEEK		8,000	8,000	8,000
121-30	BURNOUTS/CARBON/GELS						
	SERIES	1	WEEK		250	250	250
					Total for 121		12,344
122	PRODUCTION VIDEO						
122-01	TECHNICAL DIRECTOR						
	SERIES-TAPED	2	DAYS		425	850	
	PAYROLL TAX	13.85	%		850	118	
	WORKMAN'S COMP	3.10	%		850	26	994
122-02	VIDEO CONTROL						
	SERIES-TAPED	2	DAYS		375	750	
	PAYROLL TAX	13.85	%		750	104	
	WORKMAN'S COMP	3.10	%		750	23	877
122-03	CAMERA OPERATOR						
	SERIES-TAPED	2	DAYS	4	375	3,000	
	PAYROLL TAX	13.85	%		3,000	416	
	WORKMAN'S COMP	3.10	%		3,000	93	3,509
122-04	VIDEOTAPE OPERATOR						
	SERIES-TAPED	2	DAYS		350	700	
	PAYROLL TAX	13.85	%		700	97	
	WORKMAN'S COMP	3.10	%		700	22	

GOOD COMPANY   Pg. 8

Acct #	Description	Amount	Units	X	Rate	Subtotal	Total
122	PRODUCTION VIDEO (Cont'd)						
							819
122-05	MAINTENANCE ENGINEER (Cont'd)						
	SERIES-TAPED	2	DAYS		400	800	800
122-07	CAMERA UTILITY						
	SERIES-TAPED	2	DAYS	2	300	1,200	
	PAYROLL TAX	13.85	%		1,200	166	
	WORKMAN'S COMP	3.10	%		1,200	37	1,403
122-08	CHYRON OPERATOR						
	SERIES-TAPED	2	DAYS		350	700	
	PAYROLL TAX	13.85	%		700	97	
	WORKMAN'S COMP	3.10	%		700	22	819
122-17	CAMERAS RENTALS						
	SERIES-TAPED	2	DAYS	4	500	4,000	4,000
122-20	TECH EQUIP RENTAL						
	CNTRL ROOM-SERIES-TAPE	2	DAYS		400	800	
	VTR-SERIES-1"	2	DAYS	2	400	1,600	
	VTR-SERIES-BETACAM	2	DAYS	4	350	2,800	
	VTR-SERIES-3/4"	2	DAYS		150	300	
	VTR-SERIES-VHS	2	DAYS		50	100	
	CHYRON-SERIES-TAPE	2	DAYS		375	750	
	MONITORS-SERIES-TAPE	2	DAYS		350	700	
	MISC EQUIPMENT-TAPE	2	DAYS		200	400	
	STILL STORE-TAPE	2	DAYS		500	1,000	8,450
					Total for 122		21,670
123	PRODUCTION SOUND						
123-01	STUDIO SOUND PACKAGE						
	SERIES-TAPED	2	DAYS		800	1,600	
	SERIES-MUSIC GROUP-TAPE	2	DAYS		300	600	2,200
123-02	SOUND MIXER						
	SERIES-TAPE	2	DAYS		425	850	
	PAYROLL TAX	13.85	%		850	118	
	WORKMAN'S COMP	3.10	%		850	26	994
123-03	A-2						
	SERIES-TAPE	2	DAYS		375	750	
	PAYROLL TAX	13.85	%		750	104	
	WORKMAN'S COMP	3.10	%		750	23	877
123-04	PA/SA MIXER						
	SERIES-TAPE	2	DAYS		400	800	

GOOD COMPANY   Pg. 9

Acct #	Description	Amount	Units	X	Rate	Subtotal	Total
123	PRODUCTION SOUND (Cont'd)						
123-04	PA/SA MIXER (Cont'd)						
	PAYROLL TAX	13.85	%		800	111	
	WORKMAN'S COMP	3.10	%		800	25	936
					Total for 123		5,006
124	TAPE STOCK						
124-01	1" TAPE STOCK						
	SERIES	5	DAYS	4	100	2,000	
	SALES TAX	6.50	%		2,000	130	2,130
124-02	3/4" TAPE STOCK						
	SERIES	1	WEEK	20	25	500	
	SALES TAX	6.50	%		500	33	533
124-04	BETACAM STOCK						
	SERIES-8 PER SHOW	1	WEEK	40	40	1,600	
	SALES TAX	6.50	%		1,600	104	1,704
124-05	VHS STOCK						
	SERIES	3	CASES		45	135	135
124-06	AUDIO STOCK						
	SERIES	1	WEEK		75	75	75
					Total for 124		4,577
125	TRANSPORTATION						
125-04	RUNNERS						
	SERIES-HEAD	1	WEEK		350	350	
	SERIES	1	WEEK		300	300	
	PAYROLL TAX	13.85	%		650	90	
	WORKMAN'S COMP	3.10	%		650	20	760
125-20	PASSENGER VAN RENTAL						
	SERIES	1	WEEK	2	225	450	450
125-46	MILEAGE ALLOWANCES						
	SERIES	1	WEEK		125	125	125
					Total for 125		1,335

GOOD COMPANY

Acct #	Description	Amount	Units	X	Rate	Subtotal	Total
131	STUDIO/STAGE RENTALS						
131-01	STAGE RENTAL						
	SERIES-TAPE	3	DAYS		2,000	6,000	
							6,000
					Total for 131		6,000
	TOTAL PRODUCTION						91,417
134	MUSIC						
134-05	MUSIC CLEARANCE						
	SERIES	1	WEEK	4	250	1,000	1,000
134-11	SYNCH LICENSES						
	SERIES	1	WEEK	4	750	3,000	3,000
134-12	MASTER/VIDEO LICENSES						
	SERIES	1	WEEK		1,000	1,000	1,000
					Total for 134		5,000
135	POST PRODUCTION VIDEO						
135-02	ON-LINE EDITING						
	SERIES-TAPE	2	HOURS	5	650	6,500	
	SERIES-CLIPS	1	HOUR	5	450	2,250	8,750
135-10	VIDEOTAPE DUPLICATION						
	SERIES	1	WEEK	20	75	1,500	1,500
135-15	BLACK & CODED STOCK						
	SERIES	1	WEEK	5	225	1,125	1,125
					Total for 135		11,375
136	POST PRODUCTION SOUND						
136-03	VOICE OVER						
	SERIES	1	HOUR		225	225	225
					Total for 136		225

GOOD COMPANY   Pg. 11

Acct #	Description	Amount	Units	X	Rate	Subtotal	Total
137	OPEN/CLOSE/BUMPER TITLES						
137-01	MAIN TITLES						
	SERIES	1	WEEK		800	800	800
					Total for 137		800
138	PURCHASE OF VISUALS						
138-01	VISUAL CLIP PURCHASE						
	SERIES		ALLOW	5	400	2,000	2,000
					Total for 138		2,000
	TOTAL POST PRODUCTION						19,400
143	GENERAL EXPENSES						
143-01	OFFICE RENTAL						
	SERIES	1	WEEK		750	750	750
143-05	LEGAL FEE/EXPENSES						
	SERIES	1	WEEK		700	700	700
143-08	COMPUTER CONSULT/SERVICE						
	SERIES	1	WEEK		80	80	80
143-09	COMPUTER & SOFTWARE PURCH						
	SERIES	1	WEEK		150	150	150
143-10	TELEPHONE & COMMUNICATION						
	SERIES	1	WEEK		1,200	1,200	1,200
143-11	OFFICE XEROX						
	SERIES	1	WEEK		600	600	600
143-12	POSTAGE						
	SERIES	1	WEEK		200	200	200
143-20	OFFICE SUPPLIES						
	SERIES	1	WEEK		250	250	250
143-22	OFFICE EQUP/RENTAL & SERV						
	SERIES	1	WEEK	6	20	120	120
143-23	FURNITURE RENTAL/PURCHASE						
	SERIES	1	WEEK		200	200	200
143-26	AUDIO/VIDEO EQUIP RENTAL						
	SERIES	1	WEEK	3	400	1,200	1,200
143-31	VIDEOTAPE STORAGE						
	SERIES	1	WEEK		75	75	

GOOD COMPANY

Acct #	Description	Amount	Units	X	Rate	Subtotal	Total
143	GENERAL EXPENSES (Cont'd)						
143-31	VIDEOTAPE STORAGE (Cont'd)						75
143-50	BANK CHARGES						
	SERIES	1	WEEK		30	30	30
143-80	OFFICE WATER						
	SERIES	1	WEEK		25	25	25
						Total for 143	5,580
144	INSURANCE						
144-01	GENERAL LIABILITY						
	SERIES	1	WEEK		275	275	275
144-02	ENTERTAINMENT PACKAGE						
	SERIES	1	WEEK		450	450	450
144-03	ERRORS & OMMISSIONS						
	SERIES	1	WEEK		450	450	450
144-08	NON-OWNED AUTO						
	SERIES	1	WEEK		45	45	45
144-09	GUILD FLIGHT						
	SERIES	1	WEEK		30	30	30
						Total for 144	1,250
145	MISCELLANEOUS						
145-01	PACKAGING FEE						
	AGENCY PACKAGING FEE		ALLOW		12,500	12,500	
	5% OF BUDGET ($250,000)						12,500
145-02	CONTINGENCY						
	10% BELOW THE LINE		ALLOW		12,900	12,900	
	NOT INCL PKGING FEE						12,900
						Total for 145	25,400
	TOTAL OTHER						32,230
	TOTAL ABOVE-THE-LINE						108,575
	TOTAL BELOW-THE-LINE						143,047
	ABOVE & BELOW-THE-LINE						251,621
	TOTAL FRINGES						21,675
	GRAND TOTAL						251,621

WHAT HAPPENS NEXT?

The Pick-Up

There are a few factors you cannot control even when a pilot or run-thru is sold and financed by a studio or network. These are the changes of direction that occur on a seemingly weekly basis, especially when ratings are low, advertising rates are weak, and certain executives "take the hit" for the bad times. Just as an executive producer can lose his job when ratings begin to fall, network and studio executives suffer the same fate.

I have lost the *pick-up*—in this case, pick-up means selecting the show to go on the air—of a number of shows because of an executive losing his job. I will share one experience with you. After becoming known for producing magazine programs, I decided to combine my reputation with the reputation of one of the famous women's print magazines. The magazine with which I made a deal was *Woman's Day*, and I sold two pilots, run-thrus, to NBC for a truly measly $35,000. However, these shows did not require a large staff, musical production numbers, or a complex set.

We did two shows with two different female hosts in a small studio in Glendale, hardly the prestigious section of the production community. In fact, one of my memories of the facility was that it had a washing machine just offstage, so costumes could be washed—practical, but not what one usually finds in a high-end production facility. But it was homey and served the purpose. The audience consisted mainly of friends and relatives of the people working on the production, and the mood was informal. Everything clicked, and the then-head of daytime programming for NBC was absolutely elated. His quote was, "I can't believe that I have been throwing away millions of dollars on programming that stinks, and you've given me a hit for $35,000." There were the Hollywood handshakes, grabs of the upper arm, hugs, etc., and my partners and I thought we had just been picked up.

Our contract read that the network had thirty days to inform us in writing whether or not they were putting us on the air. On the fourteenth day, I picked up *Daily Variety* and read the headline, "Brian Frons Axed at NBC." He was our executive!

When an executive takes over the job of a disgraced executive, he must purge all projects the former executive brought to the table and begin anew. The out-going or out-gone executive's show then becomes what is known as an *orphan project* for obvious reasons. So much for a sure thing! Of course, once the show is released, the producer is free to pitch it at one of the competing networks or cable operations. However, everything is Hollywood is a matter of perception. Since NBC passed on the project, it became undesirable at CBS, ABC, and the cable networks, and the show never went to series.

Development

Once a show has been sold, it is put into "development." Producers love to announce to those they meet at restaurants, supermarkets, or even parking lots that they have "five development deals." This is a Hollywood game! The listener reacts by sounding impressed. A good "Wow!" usually does the trick. The game, though, is *everybody* knows a development deal means little. Anything could still happen.

Another way of telling someone about such a deal is, "Disney just bought my new game show." After the "Wow!" or "Fabulous," the recipient of the news asks the real question: "What was the commitment?" Rarely is this answered eagerly because it is usually less than meets the eye.

"They're putting it into development," the producer responds reluctantly. The listener then "innocently" asks, "Are they going to pilot? The hesitation grows longer. "Well, uh, we're going to do a run-thru first, and then go to pilot."

A run-thru is often a bare-bones presentation, meant to put the concept on its feet so that the buyers can determine if they want to spend bigger bucks on an actual pilot. It can also be used in place of a pilot. A run-thru can even take the form of a non-taped stage presentation or a video done with no scenery.

Dozens of projects go in and out of development this way. The home run occurs when so many buyers want a show that the producer can demand a full pilot. Only at this point does the executive producer receive anything beyond minimal payment. All of the research, travel, sales, and negotiations have resulted *only* in expenses, not in earnings. It is the *hope* a show will get on the air and become a hit that the executive producer is counting on. However, it is not unusual to go from development deal to development deal and not get picked up for pilot. At other times, pilots are shot but are then rejected as a series. Keep in mind, the salary the executive producer receives during pilot production still barely compensates for time and effort expended.

Even after a show and a producer survive all the traps that can befall any project and receive a "green light," the extent of the commitment from the buyer is still not known. During television's earlier days, these "pick-ups" meant a great deal more than they do today. Of course, you must be excited when you have gone past the sales, development, run-thru, and pilot stages to receive word that the show will actually go into production and be aired. The next questions are how many shows are "guaranteed" and will they "pay you off" for the episodes not aired if the initial ratings are not good and the show is never seen again? This happens often.

You have seen in recent seasons the incredible hyping of the debut of a show. It debuts, then immediately "tanks" and is never seen again after the first broadcast. In the case of a non-fiction program such as the *Roseanne* talk show several years ago, every station that bought the program from the supplying company, King World (producers of *Oprah, Jeopardy!*, and *Wheel of Fortune*, had to commit to a two-year *pay or play* deal. What does this mean? Pay or play means that the station agrees to buy and pay for the program for two years. If, for some reason, the station wants to take the show off its schedule before the two-year commitment has been fulfilled, the station still has to pay the balance of the money owed.

Often, because of the financial commitment, a station will run a show even though the ratings are dreadful. In the case of the *Roseanne* talk show, however, all of the NBC affiliate stations begged King World to take the show off the air after the first year. King World had tremendous clout because of its many successes and the power to say "absolutely not." However, the ratings for the show were so abysmal—the show was destroying the ratings for the rest of their daytime schedules—that NBC stations decided not to air the show, even though they had to pay King World for the remaining year. By the end of the run, the show was still being taped, but hardly any stations were carrying it—and King World still made a profit!

While a "power player" like King World can get away with these tactics, the individual executive producer cannot. He is only "as good as his last show." With conglomerates like Viacom, AOL TimeWarner, Disney, NBC/Universal, and Fox owning nearly the entire television industry, a single enemy at only one entity of the conglomerate can result in your being rejected by the entire company. If you disappoint or make an enemy at each of the above companies, you have effectively left the producing business in Hollywood! Therefore, as soon as the show is picked up, the executive producer must go into battle mode. He must hire the best staff, director, scenic designer, and lighting director available and make a deal with a production facility offering the most for the given budget.

The executive producer hires all personnel and approves everything from the theme music to the *graphic look*—colors and fonts that define the background look for all text—to the design or redesign of the set, always maintaining a single vision of what the show will be like when all the elements are integrated.

Some concepts work and some don't. If they don't, it is not the fault of the individual in charge of that department—it is, instead, the fault of the executive producer. Unless that individual has the creativity, taste, and understanding to know exactly what will and won't work, the show will probably fail. Even if the show initially succeeds but is not what the buyers, stations, and advertisers perceived it to be, the executive producer will be gone.

Executive producers who are gone at the outset of a program immediately enter "limbo land." If they are fortunate, they may get a chance to move on to other projects. However, everyone talks in Hollywood. Rumors run rampant about who will be fired or why someone has been fired. These rumors can stop executives from risking their jobs by hiring that executive producer. Every executive producer is allowed a flop after many successes (just as a movie star is), but after two or three failures, even top players—such as the actress Demi Moore—lose their standing and find themselves part of the history rather than the future of the industry.

Let us say, however, that the executive producer has done an outstanding job of envisioning the program, has hired the right personnel, and had his vision received well by the network or studio. He now has the job of delivering the show on either a daily or weekly basis and is responsible for the consistency of its quality. Should that quality falter or the ratings drop (which indicates that the public believes the quality has faltered), the executive producer must "scapegoat" in order to delay his own execution. Therefore, staff members may be replaced, directors may be replaced, the format may be altered—even the theme music *or opening animation* (music and title sequence) may be redone. The executive producer must constantly acknowledge weaknesses, demonstrate both creative and personal flexibility by making the necessary changes, and show that he is not locked into a narrow vision of a show. If the executive producer is lucky enough to have a hit, he must begin each new season by freshening up the look, quickening the pace, changing everything that's not working, and adding new features. In general, the necessity to prove one's self never ends.

The Run-Thru

Because the head of NBC daytime programming knew my track record with magazine formats, he committed to a run-thru of my new show *Daytime*. I was given only $85,000 for the run-thru when a pilot for the same show would have cost between $400,000-$500,000. One would think that my run-thru would have a minimal set, modest production values, and be—at most— an *idea* of what the show would look like produced for the actual budget.

Wrong! I sensed from the beginning that, if I were to convince executives to try something other than the same old talk-show format, I could leave nothing to their imaginations.

Fixing the Details

First, I hired Bill Bohnert, a scenic designer who had worked for me before and whose career went back to *The Ed Sullivan Show*. Since there was no money to design and build a new set for this show, Bill scrounged through scenic shops to find scenic elements from canceled shows that he could pull together into a workable design.

Next, the band. What was I going to do about a band? I wanted at least six pieces with a hip band leader to look contemporary. In that way, I would attract that all-important eighteen to forty-nine-year-old demographic. The solution? I hired a group of actors at fifty dollars apiece who had absolutely no idea how to play the musical instruments I rented. However, with the right bandleader and by shooting the band from a distance, no one could see that they weren't actually playing. I used recorded music so the show had "the right sound" based on the music selections I chose. It is important to note that I could take liberties with musical *licensing rights*—the agreement between the licenser and the user to establish the cost for a song—since this show would never be aired.

By the time the executive came to the taping of the show, I expected him to be flabbergasted by the beautiful set, live band, and high quality of the production, which looked as if it were ready to premiere on national television. Instead, he entered, nodded approvingly but nominally, and retreated to the *green room*, the backstage furnished room, complete with refreshments, where the performers and executives watch the show. The show went well, with a strong musical number, funny interactions between the hosts, and a strong reaction from the audience, in the historic studio where *I Love Lucy* and *Burns and Allen* filmed their episodes. Everyone felt the electricity of a hit in the air, and the executive left after congratulating us.

About a week later I was told that *Daytime* was a definite for the NBC daytime schedule. On the day the decision-makers for NBC were to meet, everyone felt encouraged, but I had been around too long not to realize that even a definite can be a crap-shoot. Later that same day, I received the dreaded call. The show had been on the schedule until the last ten minutes of the meeting, when they decided that no one knew Bob Goen and were not sure that viewers were ready for the return of music to daytime television. Instead, the network selected a program that lasted only thirteen weeks. Bob Goen, as I said earlier, became the now-famous host of *Entertainment Tonight*, and about a year later, Rosie O'Donnell successfully brought talk/variety back to television.

4
THE SHOW RUNNER'S WEEKLY SCHEDULE

SCHEDULING: THE KEY TO SUCCESS

I could never have succeeded in the pressure-cooker world of producing difficult shows without having spent many years perfecting the minute-to-minute, day-to-day, and week-to-week tasks of being the show runner of *Hour Magazine*. By the time *Hour Magazine* went on the air in September 1980, I had already spent a year and a half preparing the show and the host through his trial months in Philadelphia, Boston, and San Francisco. Now that *Hour Magazine* was ready to go on the air, I suddenly had 200 shows a year to produce—six every three days, five weeks out of six. It took me most of the first year to establish patterns to guarantee every show could be delivered on time and on budget.

Early on, I realized that the key to being a successful show runner was consistency. Every deadline, every meeting, every script, every booking, every rehearsal had to be at the same time every day, every week, and every year. Predictability had to be so great that, if the clock said 3:40 P.M. on Thursday, you knew that you would find me in the stage-right wing where the TelePrompTer was located. Our schedule was that exact: Forty staff members and twenty-five crewmembers were synchronized into a single cohesive organization. Shows were taped nearly every Wednesday, Thursday, and Friday at noon and 4:00 P.M. Overtime began at 6:01 P.M.

How was this accomplished? It began with the creation of a grid—a sample of which follows—for the six shows scheduled each week. Each of the seven segments of each the six episodes had its own square inch. Six weeks worth of grids were prepared at any one time and, since this was the eighties, they were all typed on an electronic typewriter—and often! At least once an hour, a new grid was prepared and distributed among the entire staff. Any change would be asterisked so that everyone was kept informed and up to date.

Because we taped Wednesday through Friday, Monday and Tuesday were the hectic workdays. Since more than eighty percent of my staff remained with me during the seven years I produced *Hour Magazine,* they knew I liked to handle stress with intense work and a good dose of humor. After all, we were making a television show, not finding the cure for a major disease. We all went into television because it seemed like fun. I had seen during my *Dinah!* days how perverse and dysfunctional a staff could become under a vicious leader and was determined to keep the mood upbeat, even when we found ourselves two hours before show time with a large gaping hole when a major guest dropped out. When we faced such a crisis, I would gather my troops. The rate of my speech would triple, and within minutes, everyone was mobilized and given an assignment. The assignments were prioritized and, if a lower priority seemed to solve our problem first, I would give it a five- to fifteen-minute period before I committed to it as a solution. Never did a crisis go unsolved during all of those years because we were an ensemble, and I was proud to be the leader of that ensemble. I believe that the joy a staff feels in a positive environment is reflected back onto the show. And the viewing audience does sense all of this.

A TYPICAL WEEK

By taping six shows a week instead of five, we were able to tape not only an entire week of episodes, but also one additional episode to keep in reserve. The first additional show would be a Monday show;

the second a Tuesday show—and so on. In that way, we produced more episodes in fewer weeks, which resulted in tremendous savings.

So, at any one time in a typical week, I would be looking at the grids for six weeks of shows, or a total of thirty-six shows, in addition to supervising the conception, development, and production of new episodes in the series. The shows became so ingrained in my head that I could quote a future show number and recite everything booked for that show—without looking at the grid. I truly lived each show as it was put through production and then post-production.

Scripts for shows for the following week, each of which I read before they went to the script typist, were due by the end of the day on Friday. The formula for each show was that it had to have a story with an emotional element, a celebrity with a story to tell, a remote feature, and at least one light demonstration piece. I juggled the order of these segments until each program had the best flow. If a segment was dropped and replaced by a lesser segment, that segment was scheduled during the second half hour. The first twenty minutes of each show were crucial since it was during that time that viewers decided to stay with us, go to a soap opera, or check out the competitors.

Preparation Days: Monday and Tuesday

Monday

Scripts were distributed by 9:00 A.M. on Monday morning, along with the up-to-the-minute grids so everyone knew what we had, and what was missing.

At 9:30, I met with the segment producers to go through each segment of each of the six shows. During this time, the segment producer described every move, every question, and every surprise planned, and then faced scrutiny about whether these were the best segments possible. If a celebrity interview had become too familiar and predictable, I demanded a hook, and we would all contribute ideas until the interview had its own character and uniqueness.

When appropriate, I would call in the research coordinator to ask for more material about a celebrity guest. I required each celebrity interview deal with an aspect of that individual's personality not covered in other interviews. Authors were not allowed to show the covers of their

	Show #636 AIR DAY – MON LARRY	Show #637 AIR DAY – TUES KAREN	Show #638 AIR DAY – WED MARGIE	
	WED #1 5/9 (5/28)	WED #2 5/9 (5/29)	THUR #1 5/10 (5/30)	
1	SYLVESTER STALLONE PART 1 (TAPED BEFORE #638) (I'M A NEW MAN) ___ KC	SYLVESTER STALLONE: P2 (TAPED BEFORE #638) (MY SPECIAL RELATIONSHIP W/MY SON) ___ KO	SYLVESTER STALLONE PART 3 * ___ LF	
2	DR. LORAINE STERN (HOTTEST MEDICAL BREAKTHROUGHS FOR CHILDREN) ___ LF	B O N N I E (STUDIO) RIGHTS OF FATHERS WHO PAY CHILD SUPPORT JAMES COOK ___ MF	B O N N I E **LIVING DANGEROUSLY** MOMS WORKING WITH GANGS ___ CP	
3	BONNIE OLYMPIC HOPEFULS (SYNCHRONIZED SWIMMERS) ____	WIDOW EXERCISE (SHIRLEE FONDA) ___ LFR	GRAND PRIZE WINNING PETS HORUS, RICK CARRIER, LAZAR THE WONDER DOG, TOM ROCZEN, JEEPY, OREO, MR. LUCKY ___ LFC	
4	ROSALYNN CARTER (I MISS THE WHITE HOUSE) ____ MF	R E M O T E WOMAN WHO IS ALLERGIC TO EVERYTHING ___	LA TOYA JACKSON (IT'S A THRILLER BEING MICHAEL JACKSON'S SISTER) ___ PA	
5	BETTY THOMAS (*HILL STREET BLUES*) (I'M OFF THE STREETS) (TAPED AFTER #635aa) ____ LFR	DR. WILLIAM RADER (SEX IS IMPORTANT IN MARRIAGE) ___ CP	DR. ROSENFELD'S FILE: MEDICAL UPDATE #40 (HERPES WARNING)(TAPED AFTER #625z) ___ MF	
6	LAURIE BURROWS GRAD (SENSUOUS CHEESECAKES) (TAPED AFTER #640) ____ LF	MARJORIE REED (AN ENTERTAINING SHOWER) ___ MF	FATHER'S DAY FASHIONS (TAPED AFTER #603) CHIP TOLBERT ___ LF	

7	(TAPED AFTER #640)
	WINDOW
	  BYE ___
	LF
		WINDOW
		  BYE ___
		MF
			(TAPED AFTER #603)
			WINDOW
			  BYE ___
			LF	

	BANK: SHOW (#635) MISSING CHILDREN SPECIAL (CP)	BONNIE: NATURAL MOTHER WINS BACK CHILDS (#640AA)(CPD)	BANK: SYLVESTER STALLONE & DOLLY PARTON (FIVE PARTS) (KC)	

Show #639 (END SW) AIR DAY – THRS KAREN	Show #640 AIR DAY – FRI LARRY	Show #640AA AIR DAY – THRS ARGIE
THUR #2 5/10 (5/31)	FRI #1 5/11 (6/1)	FRI #2 5/11 (7/5)
MR. AND MRS. MILTON BERLE PART 1 * (TAPED BEFORE #640) ——— LF	MR. AND MRS. MILTON BERLE PART 2 * ——— LF	DEBBI MORGAN (*ALL MY CHILDREN*) (WHY I'M SINGLE AGAIN) ——— MFR
B O N N I E (STUDIO) **LOVE STORY** **COUPLES REUNITED AFTER AUSCHWITZ** HANNA & WALKER KOMER ——— MFC	HARVEY LEVIN (DO YOU KNOW YOUR RIGHTS? QUIZ) ——— MF	B O N N I E (STUDIO) BIOLOGICAL MOTHER WINS BACK CHILD (TAPED AFTER $640aa) PATTY COCHRANE; HELEN RAMIREZ ——— CP
DR. ROBERT MENDELSOHN (HOW TO KEEP YOUR CHILD HEALTHY – IN SPITE OF YOUR DOCTOR) ——— MF	B O N N I E A FAMILY OF WOMEN CLOWNS ——— CP	LIZ SMITH (ON REMOTE) ——— MF
R E M O T E SOAP BOX DERBY FAMILY	NEW AT HOME MEDICAL TESTS (DR. DAVID SOBEL) ——— CP	SINGLE AGAIN AFTER 50 KAREN FRITTS SHIRLEY BERNSTEIN ——— KC
FOUR LOVERS A NIGHT (TAPED AFTER #634) DR. PATRICK CARNES, RUTH, SALLY ——— MFL	FARM FOR "GROWING BABIES" * KATHERINE WYCKOFF, BRENDA ——— KC	R E M O T E MALE PMS CLINIC ————
HOUR COOKBOOK CHARO (CUCHI CUCHI COOKING) ——— KCR	**SHAPING UP** TWIN SHAPE-UP (BROUGH TWINS, CANDI, RANDI) ——— LFR	**HOUR COOKBOOK** TONI TENNILLE ——— LF

WINDOW
    BYE ———
KCC
	WINDOW
	    BYE ———
		WINDOW
		BYE
		———

BANK: CINDY ADAMS (LF) #648) JOEY GAYLE OLINEKOVEA (KC) (#643)	BANK: MR & MRS. M. BERLE (#639) (LF) LAURIE GRAD (#636,#641)(LF)	BANK: NATHANIEL BRANDEN (R)

books—otherwise the show would have looked like a series of commercials —but a plug for a film or book could be given in the introduction and, possibly, again in the close. I would edit out any additional references if the celebrity attempted to "torpedo" me on camera. Senator Edward Kennedy practiced the most creative and media savvy method of overcoming that restriction. Gary mentioned the name of Kennedy's book in his introduction, but did not show a copy of the book. At the end of the interview, while Gary was thanking him, Kennedy whipped out the book and pointed it directly at the camera covering him. The result: The book received a close-up. I had to admire Kennedy's determination and the charm with which he accomplished his goal.

Motion picture clips were shown sparingly. I felt they were useless when taken out of context and hated the audience's applauding what they obviously did not understand. Psychologists who wrote books about anything from menopause to child murderers had to bring a case study if they expected to talk about their findings. For example, the psychologist would have to supply at least one preteen murderer to appear on the show if he were discussing that subject. This was more compelling television. I am often shocked by highly praised shows, such as *Today*, that allow authors to blather on about the findings of their studies without insisting on the human element. What keeps a viewer hooked is what the person who has lived the life is saying.

Are you beginning to understand that the show runner not only runs the show, but also determines policy? I considered myself easy to work with and always—usually—was pleasant to everyone. However, no one was going to compromise my beliefs about what the show was to be, and one of the things it was going to be was a service show for women, not a long, sycophantic commercial for anyone. I felt my responsibility was to my show and my viewing audience, rather than to any "user" who offered me a free lunch or insincere friendship. An appearance on *Hour Magazine* sold about 35,000 books and I used that as leverage to keep commercialism under control. I insisted that more books would be sold if viewers didn't channel surf but were instead riveted to the screen.

We also regularly discussed series for the next "sweeps shows." *Sweeps* months are November, February, and May, along with a less-important July. The ratings during those months determine the price of commercials for the next quarter. If those months exhibit rating declines, commercial prices decline and, as a result, stations examine whether or not they could make more money with another show. Therefore, the goal is to produce programming for these months that is highly promotable. Promoting a series is called *stunting,* which translates into producing a series that lasts an entire week or month. For example, we did a series called "The Music of Our Lives," which featured one singer each day who sang the song that had made him famous. Patti Page sang "Tennessee Waltz"; Johnny Ray sang "Cry"; Eddie Fisher sang "Oh My Papa" (he used cue cards); and Dion sang "Abraham, Martin, and John" within that particular series. The audience tuned in and stayed tuned in.

By the time the 9:30 Monday production meeting ended at 11:15, we had discussed each elements of each of the six shows and, armed with many suggestions and changes, the segment producers left to rewrite.

The next time cue to be hit was at 1:00 P.M. when I met with the *1st PA* (who was also known as the Booth PA). The PA was my "left arm"—because I'm left-handed—and was in charge of making sure all production elements needed by the segment producers, such as props, photos, videotapes, video clips, etc., were in hand. The segment producers had so much to handle that they sometimes forgot. But there is no time or patience for forgetfulness in the world of daily television.

In preparation for my meeting with the 1st/Booth PA, segment producers had to submit *bumper* suggestions—music, text, and video to tease the next segment before or after commercials. I was always looking for clever phrases that would attract viewers' curiosity. For instance, we did a weekly cooking feature on Mondays called "Make It Easy," with Laurie Burrows Grad, with a bumper that usually featured the song "Let's Make It Nice and Easy."

The classic "bad music suggestion" came in connection with a segment about breast cancer detection. It was a given that serious segments had generic music and basic text. However, this particular segment producer suggested we play the song "Feelings" during the breast cancer detection bumper. That segment producer was fired at the end of the season.

Often the segment producers were so busy trying to pre-interview their guests and put together the elements of production that the 1st/ Booth PA and I spent two hours trying to choreography each of the six shows ahead. We assigned times to each segment, knowing that the *TRT—total running time* of the show—was 45:45 (45 minutes and 45 seconds). We also assigned sections of the stage for each segment, assigned *call times*—the times by which each guest had to arrive—and *taping order*—sometimes a guest had other commitments and had to tape out of order. It was during these two-hour periods that the show was truly produced—I began to see each show for its strengths and weaknesses. As a result, I often had to leave the PA meeting and hold an impromptu meeting with segment producers and researchers to initiate any necessary changes. Additions, deletions, and substitutions were constantly being made.

Later that afternoon, while the resulting rundowns were being typed and distributed by the PA, and while production elements were being arranged and coordinated with the prop director/scenic decorator, the pace really quickened. We were just thirty-six hours from production on the first of our six episodes. As this was happening, executive producer Marty Berman and I would jump in a car and drive to Burbank from Hollywood, where we would meet with Group W president Ed Vane and his henchman, George Resing. These guys didn't have a clue about what women wanted to see on television and, after years in the industry on the programming side, had no idea how television was actually produced. However, I knew my role in this Monday meeting: I had to sell the spots we were doing that week.

In preparation for the meeting, I would work with my assistant to redo the grid so that every segment sounded like a headline from *The National Enquirer*. Even Vane and Resing would laugh when I put my comedy background to use. My titles, along with joke-laden patois, kept them amused and generally got me through the meeting with no trouble. Marty would sit there quietly while I did my comedy act. Finally, Vane would say, "Sounds like a good week," and we were home-interference-free. That was when the ratings were good! When the ratings dropped from the week before, my jokes fell flat, and there was talk about "shaking up the show." Translation: Fire some people or else get fired yourself! I would get a twinge in the pit of my stomach when the word *stale* was injected into the conversation. I had developed a tremendous camaraderie with my staff, and did not want to have to offer up sacrifices in the name of improving the show. However, and this was rare good fortune in the run of any show, the ratings held up for most of the eight years I produced, and I managed to make minimal changes to the staff.

Tuesday

Tuesday mornings began with a 9:00 A.M. research meeting. All five researchers would pitch the hundred or so best ideas they had culled from what was probably at least a thousand pitches received via phone and mail. They had also read every newspaper and magazine around the country for unique stories with which we could run and add our journalistic mark. I am proud to say that, through our producing and research staffs, we were the first media organization to do stories about what eventually became known as AIDS, the benefits of lumpectomy as an alternative to mastectomy in certain cases, the announcement about toxic shock syndrome from tampons (which became a major story in the 1980s), and the legitimacy of PMS (Pre-Menstrual Syndrome) as a medical condition.

By the end of the meeting at 11:00 A.M., we were all exhausted. After listening to each pitch, I would ask who the spokesperson was to be, ask to see the tape—and evaluate it if we had viewed it at the meeting—decide which stories to pursue, and discuss the status of segments that had previously been pitched. Before any booking was made, I requested a second opinion to avoid buyer's remorse. If everyone agreed a booking should take place, we moved forward. If, however, a segment producer saw a potential problem regarding a subject or guest, I would meet with both parties in my office, hear all sides, and either make a decision or bring a decisive third party—usually another segment producer—into the mix.

Throughout the day, my intercom kept ringing and people streamed in and out to update me about bookings, to confirm dates, and to discuss date conflicts. We were constantly being given a new color-coded grid with the date and time it was issued.

On Tuesday afternoons at 1:00 P.M. we had the most crucial meeting of the week—the production meeting—attended by the director, associate director, 1st/Booth PA, property master/set decorator, costumer, segment producers, and script typist. Each segment producer read his segment out loud while the director took notes about how I wanted it to be shot, along with special instructions for the director's crew, including stage managers, cameramen, audio mixer, lighting directors, TelePrompTer technician, grips (stagehands), *TD* (the technical director is the person who punches the buttons that switch cameras to produce the effects), and the *Chyron* operator—the person who types the text into the computer, to which the TD adds graphics.

Chyron has almost become a generic term, such as Kleenex or Xerox, for the machine that creates the text to identify guests and the bumpers. The Chyron operator also builds text to support information given in the segment. For example, if a physician were to announce the five major symptoms of heart disease, the Chyron operator would type in the preapproved material exactly as written by the segment producer. This information would then be placed within a *mortis*—frame—by the TD, who knew all the "looks" stored on the computer system that gave consistency to the show.

During that Tuesday meeting, each of the forty-two segments to be taped during the next three days was discussed. I also had to coordinate the order in which a guest would discuss a topic with what was built on the Chyron. As you will notice on *Good Morning, America, Today,* or any similar show, the prebuilt Chryon matches the order in which a guest discusses her topic. Otherwise, the show would look poorly produced. Therefore, *everyone* and *everything* must be coordinated, so there are no miscues.

Any anticipated production problem was also discussed. Solutions were encouraged from all staff members: Everyone had the right to express an opinion without fear of reprisal, but, as show runner, the final decision, the final responsibility, was mine.

One problem for discussion might be whether a future celebrity guest might appear too frail to make an entrance. One such frail guest was TV pioneer Arthur Godfrey, then in his eighties. He limped even during his peak as a television star and was rarely seen walking. However, he was too important to pre-set—have the guest seated on stage when the segment begins. We decided to have him, and other similarly frail stars, take one step into camera frame to the chair as the audience applauded. It was the perfect solution, providing practicality while respecting the guest and his infirmities. As it turned out, taping—in what would be Godfrey's last public appearance—was delayed for half an hour while he struggled with respiratory problems in a special portable dressing room. We were not sure if we were going to tape a segment with him or be forced to call the paramedics.

Another example of protecting the dignity of a guest occurred when Rock Hudson entered the studio looking gaunt and, obviously, very ill. This was before he made the announcement that he was suffering from AIDS. Instead of giving him a grand entrance through the french doors, which would have shocked the audience and humiliated Hudson, we pre-set him to limit the visibility of the ravages of the disease. Although nothing was said, he appeared to be grateful for the decision.

We also had to deal with celebrities who came with their own set of demands. For instance, the audience was used to seeing Gary Collins in the "den" set looking to his right, since he photographed better from that side in that particular set. This meant that his guests sat to his right, facing left. Sophia Loren, however, insisted on being shot from the right side only. Obviously, we had to accommodate her, since she was an outstanding booking. I told Gary that he would have to sacrifice his better side for the interview. Gary was always gracious about such requests.

Sometimes we produced "reunion" segments. These were segments in which relatives or former lovers who had not seen each other for fifty or more years were reunited on stage for the first time. These popular segments took a great deal of planning because, if the two parties ran into each other backstage, the entire surprise element would be spoiled. As a result, the choreography of each participant, from arrival on the studio lot to the moment the camera watched loved ones reunite with hopes of an emotionally charged moment, had to be planned with military precision. Many people worked in concert to make sure that there was no possibility of error. Of course, the guests' reactions at the moment of meeting were completely unscripted and unpredictable: They ranged from hugs and tears of happiness to unstoppable crying— some of which had to be edited out to fit the hour formant—to just a shrug and a "hi." When that happened, I would shake my head in disbelief. All that work for a non-reaction!

Nothing went unsaid during that two-hour Tuesday production meeting, including cautions about guests whose performances were in doubt and how we would rearrange the continuity of the show if we decided to send a particular guest to videotape heaven. If a guest was dealing with emotionally sensitive issues, I would make it clear to my director, Glen Swanson, just how I wanted it shot. I first met Glen when he was the director of *Dinah!* Although he was a fine director, who had always specialized in the musical/variety format, I rode him through my headset during a taping if he was being too polite during emotionally charged moments. I wanted the camera in extreme close-up on the eyes of the guest before they swelled with tears. That was what the audience wanted to see, and Glen would often incur my wrath when he shot those magical moments as if he were in the bleachers. Those tears were my "ratings moments."

The Tuesday production meeting ended at 3:00 P.M. Then the tension really began to rise. More often than not, we were facing several holes, where celebrities had dropped out. When the talent coordinator appeared at my door, and before she even opened her mouth, I could always tell when she was about to drop a bomb. From the talent coordinator to the researchers to the segment producers, I learned the six most awful words I could hear—and I heard them often—were "Steve, I've got some bad news." When a celebrity "dropped," which is short for "dropped out," I would call an emergency meeting with the talent coordinator and segment producers for suggestions. After the meeting, everyone including the talent coordinator would check with their contacts from managers and agents to *Celebrity Service*—an inordinately expensive daily subscription service that reports the comings and goings of celebrities. We paid thousands a year for the privilege of being able to call that service for the best and quickest route to any celebrity at a moment's notice. Every show that uses celebrities must subscribe to Celebrity Service. We even scoured other stages on the studio lot to see if anyone worth having was there. Ted Knight, who taped *Too Close for Comfort* a few studios down the street, was always amenable to be a last-minute guest, and was a delight. If we couldn't get anyone else, we used a "banked" celebrity interview.

Taping Days: Wednesday through Friday

Wednesday through Friday

Taping days—Wednesdays, Thursdays, and Fridays—were exactly the same, because precision and continuity are the keys to survival in this business. Everyone who was in the Tuesday meeting would meet again in my office at 8:45 A.M. (not 8:46 A.M.) on production days, Wednesday through Friday. Latecomers were publicly but gently chided. Habitual lateness necessitated a private meeting and a dressing down. All elements for the day's two shows—one taped at noon and the other taped at four—were "talked down" again. All names on the rundown were checked for spelling, and the titles that described them were dissected and often changed before they were typed into the Chyron. Every change from the previous day was announced, along with the ramifications of those changes. An exact schedule for the day, which gave the order of rehearsal times for *demo*—"demonstration"—segments, taping order, and times for each segment for both shows, lunch breaks, and exact times for the union five-minute breaks that the crew had to have each hour, was distributed. In essence, everyone looked at the schedule and confirmed that it was reasonable.

By 9:30, it was time to move into battle mode—at times with elements still missing, which necessitated constant hallway meetings to fill the gaps. I remember looking at the line-up of 200 people who were waiting to become members of the studio audience, and silently panicking when I did not have a full show in place. Yet they were entirely clueless!

While Glen Swanson had a meeting with his crew to talk down—going through the schedule of the day moment by moment at a pace equivalent to double-talk—the two shows and hand out special assignments, I segued into a private meeting with Gary Collins. I needed his full attention: He was often tired in the morning because of the pressures of the schedule, so I allowed no phone calls or interruptions. We had to focus on what needed to be accomplished in each segment. Gary had received the scripts via messenger on Monday morning, along with limited stacks of research. Because he did forty-two segments a week, I insisted that only essential information be sent. In addition, Gary and I reviewed every bit of information he needed to survive the six- to eight-minute segments. Since we had only half an hour to talk this all down, our level of interaction was held in a shorthand we had honed over a long period.

After the briefing for the noon show, we went downstairs for the rehearsals of the demos, mostly to set camera *shots*—setting up what each camera should focus on and deciding which camera to use at a given moment. Cooking and exercise segments can be a disaster if the talent doesn't know which camera will be shooting, and how to be positioned. I would watch the rehearsal, particularly interested if this were a new guest. If I wasn't pleased with the rehearsal, I would either require that the segment producer work with the guest, look at the possibility of shuttling the segment to videotape heaven, or send the guest home if the taping schedule was too heavy, and the segment would be a waste of time. Although I was a fair producer, I had a show that cost $13 million a year, and no one personality was going to interfere with the success or failure of my operation.

By 11:30 Gary was in makeup, lunch was being served in the green room, and the audience was being *warmed up*—taught to laugh and applaud on cue. There was a party atmosphere, specifically for the people who were new to television and nervous about telling their stories. While all of this was happening, I was constantly interfacing with my segment producers, researchers, and talent coordinators about changes to the show about to be taped, the one to be taped at four, or one to be taped next week or four weeks later.

After 11:55 A.M., Gary was introduced to a revved-up audience. He would spend a few minutes with them, joking and telling stories. They loved it, and loved him. Then it was show time. During the show, I stood just out of camera range, facing Gary and holding a dozen pieces of *oak tag*—cue cards. One cue card, with the key questions, was placed just over the shoulder of the guest, so that Gary would know what the next question was to be. His introductions were read directly from the lens, on the TelePrompTer, as though they were spontaneous. I found it particularly funny that we had to begin the copy of each show with "Hi. I'm Gary Collins. Welcome to *Hour Magazine*." When I asked Gary if we could eliminate that line from the copy, since he knew his own name and the title of the show, he said that he preferred that we did not. Oh well!

When I felt that Gary was not following up a question with one that the answer begged, I would quickly write it on the cue card with a black Magic Marker. Sometimes, I had to help him correct a gaffe. For instance, I had told him that *General Hospital* actress Jackie Zeman had been married to disc jockey Murray the K, who was sometimes referred to—mostly jokingly—as "the fifth Beatle." I also mentioned that the two of them had divorced, and Murray had recently died. Gary must have been in a funk that day, because he said to Jackie, "Now you and the famous DJ Murray the K are divorced." In a flash, I wrote a cue card that was laughed about for years afterward, and was even suggested as a possibile title for my autobiography. It said, "MURRAY IS DEAD!" Without a second's hesitation, Gary assumed a solemn expression and said, "Of course, since then Murray has passed on."

While each show played out, I was also on the phone with the 1st/ Booth PA, checking whether the show was on time, under time, or overtime, and, based on the reaction to any guest, kept revising the allotted times for each segment. For example, the now-famed hairdresser, José Eber (who was then an unknown but unique-looking Frenchman with a ponytail and a straw hat), appealed to the female audience, but was not anecdotal about his adventures in hair. Therefore, I knew I could give Gary rushed cues so that Eber's segment, which had been allotted five to six minutes, could be completed in two and a half to three minutes and give me the time I needed to bring the show in on time. José would usually complain that I was rushing him, but, in reality, he said everything that needed to be said in a shorter period of time. TV is not forgiving; it does not allow an extra twelve seconds for a particularly good show that feels "just right." The show ran 45: 45—good, bad, or middling. By nature, I am a punctual individual, usually arriving at all professional and social engagements fifteen minutes to half an hour *before* the appointed time. To this day, I don't know which came first, my sense of punctuality or the punctuality I developed because of the schedule I had to maintain producing so many episodes of television.

When, at 1:45 P.M., Gary would say his final phrase, "Don't forget—make every hour count," I would finally breathe a sigh of relief. Another episode was "put to bed." Anyone who does this type of work is always wrestling with the nightmare that the show either will not happen at all, or will go thousands of dollars over budget. Invariably, as the final credits rolled and the theme music played, a staff member would come over to say, "Steve, we've got a problem for the 4:00 show ...." And so it continued for most of the decade.

Two Hours to Air

Even with all of the days, weeks, and sometimes months of preparation for particular segments and episodes, there could be disasters if the last several hours before broadcast, as well as the hour(s) taping the broadcast, weren't handled with precision. The next two sections are devoted to these crucial times when the technical personnel, under the supervision of the director and the segment or episode producers, must turn the planning, scripting, and organizing into the segment or show the show runner has envisioned.

It is important to note the difference between the producer/executive producer and director in television and their counterparts in motion pictures. While the director in film is the person with the vision, it is the producer in television who rules the medium. Conversely, the producer for motion pictures is usually the person(s) who secures the financing. We often refer to some film directors as *auteurs*—the select few whose names define their products, such as Spielberg, Hitchcock, or Scorsese. In television, the equivalent person is the producer, people such as Norman Lear, Gary David Goldberg, or Dick Wolf. In television, the producer hires the director. The director's role is then to make the producer's vision a reality through his work with the technical crew and by his calling the shots.

Director's Meeting

We've already discussed the morning meeting in the show runner's office, which is held every taping day for a talk down—going through the schedule of the day moment by moment at a pace equivalent to double-talk. This double-talk is conducted using terminology defined in this book. Following the meeting, there are a number of ways to approach those precious few hours before the taping. Each show runner's philosophy varies slightly, depending upon the nature of the show, the needs of the talent, and the nature of that individual's hands-on approach. This book presents only my practices and approaches for a two-show day. By the time you become a show runner, you will have observed others in the same role and can decide which style results in the best product for you.

Even as the director enters the studio, several members of the technical crew have been in place and working for hours. Others with a later call have arrived just a few minutes before the director holds his morning meeting onstage. The executive in charge of production, also known as line producer, determines the crew's call time in advance. Remember, he's the one who upholds the weekly budget and lets the show runner know in which categories the budget is on target, under budget, and over budget; he also knows all the union rules for such things as breaks, lunch, child labor laws, and overtime. This person is in touch with the show runner throughout the day. Otherwise, the production could be in trouble with the unions, the law, and/or the studio that provides the money for the production.

By the time the director's meeting takes place—usually about 9:30 A.M. for a noon show—everyone involved has a copy of the rundown prepared earlier in the week with the 1st/Booth PA. By now, it has been revised to match any and all changes in programming. The rundown is "the Bible" for everyone involved in the taping, and everyone is handed a copy.

The rundown (see sample on pages 99-102) cites guest names as well as how they will be identified on the screen, the area of the stage on which they will appear, and whether or not they will be pre-set when the segment begins. For those guests who will make an entrance, the rundown states the melody to be played and a reminder that the audience needs to be *cued*—instructed to applaud. It also contains information about bumpers, projected *running time*—the length of each segment—and the total running time (TRT) through segment to the end of the show. As I've mentioned, the total running time for an hour show is about 45:45; for a half-hour show it's about 22:30. I say *about* because new shows seem to be adding more commercials and promos—ads about upcoming shows on the network or station—that are reducing the actual length of the show. If there is going to be a musical number, the rundown states whether it will be *live*—vocal and instrumentals will be performed in the studio; *track*—the musical background against which a performer will lip-sync; or *live to track*—the singer will sing live, but the instrumental will be recorded. The final item on the rundown is a list of props necessary for the segment.

The other item that everyone has before the director's meeting is the schedule for the day. Any production day faces dozens of time challenges, which necessitate a moment-to-moment schedule that must be precisely adhered to—barring any almost certain last-minute changes. Some of the issues typically addressed when creating this schedule are union rules regarding the necessity of a lunch break after a specific number of hours; the moment when one must *wrap*—release the cast and crew—or face overtime charges; the time constraints of particular celebrities based on their schedules; a demonstration that will cause the host to get messy, such as a facial treatment (these should be scheduled at the end of the taping for obvious reasons); or finally a guest who has a definite "out time"—the time she must leave. If the guest's segment is not completed or left untaped, it will leave a hole in the show, necessitating retaping those portions of the show in which the host refers to the guest.

Of course, the reality is, despite the best preparation, the schedule will be altered during the day. It was frustrating when it became imperative that two people tape at exactly the same time, and I was put in the position of losing one of them. It often took finessing, cajoling, bargaining, and even begging to convince one of the guests to remain ten minutes longer. However, as long as there was an initial schedule, the director could announce changes over the headsets as they occurred during the taping.

Who is at the director's meeting? Everyone who is not part of the *upstairs staff*—producers, researchers, administrative personnel—was there. These were the people who were going to be in the control room, the lighting room, the audio room as well as those out on the stage, and the set and prop people. The set and prop people were there the longest since they had the most to prepare in time for rehearsal. In fact, even by the time I would arrive at the studio, which was at least an hour before my morning meeting, I could already smell the delicious aromas for the cooking demonstrations and hear the technicians vacuuming the set and moving equipment into place. Onstage, a cozy Christmas set would have come to life, even though it might be the middle of August, or a sandy beach scene would have appeared even on a cold December morning. With a reality/non-fiction show, there is always fantasy.

The Control Room

Even those of you who have never been in a television studio have seen a control room. It may have been at the end of *Dateline NBC*, when the camera closes on all the people sitting in a darkly lit room looking busy (though you're not sure exactly what they're busy doing). In a control room there are lots of monitors, each with a different shot of the same show; the scene looks similar to one at Mission Control at the Houston Space Center. It is unsettling to realize that all those people are working on a program in which a host has just been saying good night to viewers.

Allow me to introduce the various people in the control room and their functions. The person who runs the *booth*—as the control room is called—is the director. In front of him are a microphone, a bank of video monitors on the board, which shows him what each camera is shooting, and a series of buttons that enable him to speak with his crew or the floor. Everyone on the floor and in the booth wears a headset, and many also have microphones, so that they can speak with the director. When the director wants to speak with the floor, it is usually to address the talent, or to give the studio audience an instruction such as, "I need about two minutes of enthusiastic applause." He is able to do this because of the *SA* microphone button, which directs his voice to the stage.

Here's another example that demonstrates what you see on air is not necessarily what was happening at the moment. The audience applauding a funny line may actually have been taped an hour after it happened—or taken from another program with a better-looking studio audience. Why would this happen? Say a celebrity told a joke and it bombed. In order to make him look better, laughter is sweetened. No one at home will know the difference, and if you, the viewer, didn't find it funny, well, obviously you have no sense of humor!

To the left of the director is the *technical director* (TD), who sits in front of a huge panel of buttons making all the effects occur. He actually presses the button that places the video from a particular camera on the air. While a director is *calling a show*—all the directions he gives during a broadcast—many of his directions are given to the TD. For example, the director may call, "Ready 2, *take* 2"—the second taped performance—or "Ready to dissolve 2, dissolve 2." In both cases, the TD knows to press the camera 2 button next and the cameraperson knows not to move his shot because it will be on the air momentarily.

For a "Ready 2, take 2" call, there will be a direct *cut*, which happens instantaneously. In "Ready to dissolve 2, dissolve 2, the *dissolve* happens slowly, as the TD moves a lever to cause the previous shot to fade while the new shot comes into focus.

The TD also controls the graphics designed for the show. Graphics designers are employed to design the graphic look. For example, a mortis, a visual template, is established for the bumpers, against which text (something like "Coming Up Next: New Fall Fashions") is displayed. The mortis might also be *translucent*—see-through—for those graphics that identify the guest currently being interviewed. These *IDs*—wording that identifies a guest, place, or object or gives support to points being made by an expert—appear in the lower part of the screen. They're also known as *mattes*, *supers*, and *lower thirds*, terms many directors use interchangeably. If the director calls out, "Super him" or "Matte him," the TD knows exactly what to do. All graphics and photos have been *still stored*—pages of saved graphics and photos to be used on the show—between the time the TD arrives and show time.

The TD takes photos from the floor, with the assistance of a cameraperson and the stage manager. Let's say that we have Ron Howard as a celebrity guest, and we show pictures of him from *The Andy Griffith Show*, as well as stills from the films he has directed. All of these are photographed, stored on tape, and marked with the exact location where they are to be inserted by the associate director.

While the TD is working on photos, the text for the graphics for a particular episode are being supplied by the 1st/Booth PA, who hands them to the CG operator or Chyron operator. The CG operator is the person who types the text into the *CG*—character generator. The CG operator, or Chyron operator, sits in the control room, usually behind the TD, and works closely with the TD to make sure that the correct text is matched with the appropriate mortis. The CG operator—like everyone else on both the crew and staff—must watch for misspellings at all times and confirm anything questionable before putting it on the still store.

Each segment/episode producer also checks the still stores for spelling and accuracy prior to the broadcast, taking any guest expert into the booth to check that the Chyrons reflect the points that expert will make on air, as well as the order in which those points will be discussed. For example, if a physician is going to talk about five ways to prevent heart disease, five Chyrons will be still stored. As a result, when the physician goes to the second point, it will look as though it has magically appeared on the screen.

A good producer also has a cue card behind the host and out-of-frame for the guest to read, so that the order of points is not inadvertently changed on air, causing a Chyron mismatch. This kind of error causes a *stop down*—the taping has to cease—and requires part or all of the segment to be retaped, causing unnecessary delays in the schedule. By the way, the show runner should also be familiar with every still store on the show. I double-checked my segment/episode producer by looking over his shoulder while the TD ran through all still stores before each broadcast.

To the right of the director is the associate director (AD). The AD is one of the people who arrives earlier than everyone else because it is his job to build the *show reel*—everything that has been prerecorded for the broadcast. This includes the opening animation, all field pieces, film clips, etc. The AD creates a cue sheet for the tape operators and TD, so that the exact location of a specific clip can be immediately marked. Of course, digital video has made this process far easier. Also the AD marks the location and order of each photo that has been stored by the TD. I usually assigned the AD the job of doing and editing my *strip*—daily—series because it was less expensive than hiring the director, and I was too busy preparing future episodes to do it. Consequently, my ADs spent the entire broadcast taking copious editing notes.

To the right of the AD is that valued associate of mine, the 1st/Booth PA. This individual understands the entire picture best, and it is she upon whom I depended to watch all the details while I was elsewhere. I was fortunate to have worked with some outstanding 1st/Booth PAs during the years that I was a show runner. In fact, the 1st/Booth PAs who weren't right for the position rarely lasted a week with me. It was too crucial a role to wait for anyone to grow into it. Too much depended on her efficiency.

Outside Central Control

Typically, there are other activities going on in several rooms adjacent to the central control room. The lighting director (LD) watches the lighting from his room, hands poised on dimmers to change the lighting according to the needs of the broadcast. The lighting assistant will be on-stage to adjust the direction of the lamps, or open or close *barn doors*—these widen or narrow the range of the lighting. The head of audio (A1) controls the audio levels from his room, coordinating with the A2, who puts portable microphones on the talent before they enter the stage and removes the equipment as the talent exits. By the way, the A2 has to place the portable microphones on "delicate" parts of the body. This job, of course, requires the right individual with the right attitude. The last thing a show runner needs is a guest complaining that the A2 has tried to "take advantage" while doing his job.

Two other rooms that are usually part of the control room suite, or at least nearby, are the "tape" room—in quotations because digital formats are used so often—and the master control room. The tape room consists of a massive group of machines that record the show. Not only is it important to tape the show the viewer sees, but also to record what some, if not all, of the cameras were focusing on throughout the show. The recording of the shots each camera took is called an *iso*—which stands for isolated camera. These recorded shots are invaluable, particularly after the show has ended, the guests have gone home, and you realize that another shot might have been a better "call" by the director or that certain shots are needed to clarify the segment. It is wonderful to have these choices rather than face an *air show*—one that goes on the air—that is not the best possible product.

The individuals in master control have the job of making sure video levels are maximized at all times. Their instruments assure nothing *strobes*—vibrates—on the eye of the viewer. For example, if someone wears a sports jacket that is a broad plaid, it could make the video too "hot"—too bright. The head of master control is constantly increasing or decreasing video levels, so that the people on-air and on the set look their best, and the viewing audience is not "blown out of their seats" by fashion faux pas. It is for this reason that men are advised to wear blue shirts rather than white, and women are strongly urged to avoid dresses in colors such as bright red. It always surprises me when I see a professional on-air with a dress in a color definitely not meant for television. I wonder what she and her producer were thinking.

It probably comes as no surprise that, as show runner, I always approved all outfits worn by talent on air. As you've already realized, there was no one thing or person that appeared on the screen that was not part of my overall responsibility.

Backstage

I have already mentioned the duties of the lighting assistant and the A2, both of whom are stationed backstage. Also backstage is the TelePrompTer operator, who types into the computer the script the host(s) will read from while speaking into the camera. A capable technician quickly learns the natural rate of speech of a particular host, and scrolls down the page at that speed, neither rushing ahead nor lagging behind the host. Of course, a good host or news anchor never appears to be reading. Instead, these professionals have the experience to make the words on *prompter*—as the TelePrompTer is called—sound fresh, as though he had just thought of them at the moment they were spoken. A good TelePrompTer operator is also flexible. Chances are great that there will be changes throughout the show, and the operator must react quickly and efficiently.

We've already mentioned the prop master and his assistant or assistants, who, depending on the complexity of the show, are stationed backstage. They are responsible for all set decorations and props, such as coffee mugs or information cards that the host holds—in short, any object used on the show or as part of the set. These individuals are constantly running between the backstage area and the stage itself to place and remove items for demo segments or other activities.

If a set has to be decorated to suit a theme or season, a set decorator is needed. When a show premieres, the original set is the creation of the scenic designer, whose job ends after she has made revisions based on the results of the first few shows. It is at that point that the set decorator supervises particular looks for musical acts, seasonal shows, or theme shows for instance. The set decorator is more of an artist than the prop master and, therefore, receives a higher salary.

The other person who works backstage is the 2nd stage manager. While the 1st stage manager is on the set from early morning through the broadcast, the 2nd is in charge of making sure that guests are placed in makeup and hair in an order appropriate for the time slot in which they will tape. He reports any backstage problems with guests, such as if a particular guest is inebriated or unhappy. Once the guest arrives, the 2ⁿᵈ contacts the segment/episode producer since that guest will need to be briefed, in this case to confirm that the questions and answers planned reflect the pre-interview information obtained on the phone. The 2ⁿᵈ stage manager also escorts the guest to the A2 to get "miked" before turning him over to the 1ˢᵗ stage manager onstage.

The Floor

Based on what you know about the activities in the control room, you get an idea why people are running on and off the stage and working at hectic paces. Sound is being set while lights are being adjusted and flowers are being arranged beside the host.

On the set, or floor, are the camera people. In the past, three to five *peds*—a camera on a pedestal—were used. Now, everyone is looking for less predictable, less stodgy shots, and, as a result, more hand-held cameras are being used. For example, compare the visual looks of Johnny Carson's *Tonight Show* and Jay Leno's *Tonight Show*. On the Carson version, all the shots were from stationary cameras that *panned*—the process of moving from left to right and vice versa—and *trucked*—the process of moving across the floor. No unusual angles were used, just different views of the host, the guests, and the set. However, on the Leno version, the opening is reflective of a younger feel. The *steadicam*—a camera that one can run with while maintaining a stable shot—jets up and down the aisles of the audience, while Kevin Eubanks is seen at a *Dutch angle*—pictured on an angle. The picture can even turn completely upside down. The feeling that is imparted is frenetic and fun, and considered more modern in approach. As a result, the simple three-camera show has become obsolete, as are directors who are unable to update their approach.

So let's say that we're working on a five-camera show, with two ped cameras, two hand-helds, and a *jib*—this camera is attached to a pole that rises in the air and flies around quickly, giving a sense of height and speed. In addition to the camera people, one to two *utility crew members* do anything, but mostly move cable.

Let's return to the person who is in charge of the stage during a taping day—the 1ˢᵗ stage manager. The 1ˢᵗ stage manager is always on headset, so he can follow the wishes of the director from the booth. In addition, the stage manager cues the talent when the director yells,

"Cue him"; gives time cues to let the host know how much time is left until a commercial; and conducts the rehearsal so the schedule is followed. The rundown is the stage manager's guide. A stage manager who takes control while keeping the atmosphere from becoming tense is a tremendous asset to the production. As show runner, I would work with the stage manager to give the talent a *short cue*—the short cue indicated that I wanted to get out in less time than had originally been planned—as well as other last-minute instructions that required instant reactions. Being a stage manager is not for the inflexible.

The Rehearsal

Now that you have met all the players on the crew, you know who was at the director's morning meeting. While the director was doing the talk down with the crew, I would be briefing the talent. Both our sessions would finish at about the same time, and the talent and I would go to the stage for *camera blocking*—rehearsals of segments that require agreement between the director and talent as to which camera will be used.

I would stand by while the director was on the floor with the host and guest as they went through the script with appropriate props on a *roll table*—this is just what it seems, and is great for a daily show because everything on it can be prepared in advance and rolled out without delaying the taping process. The prop master has had made all necessary signage, such as the number of calories in each of the ingredients in a cooking demonstration. The director might then rehearse how the guest is to hold up a demonstration item while talking to the host. Although the position the talent is in may appear awkward-looking in person, it guarantees that the viewer will actually see what is going on. There is nothing worse than watching a demonstration and missing it because it is never centered in the shot. If that does happen (and it can even in the best-rehearsed segments), we later do *pickups*—getting the shots that were missed and inserting them into the tape during the editing process. By doing a pickup, a shot is "cleaner" and does not look like a mistake.

While I watched the rehearsal, I would get a sense about what might not work—perhaps the guest was nervous, lacked experience, and might not "deliver." As a result, I could tell the segment/episode producer to work with that guest while telling the 1st/Booth PA that I wanted to revise the timings for each segment, beginning by reducing the guest's allotted time.

After the camera blocking, we did a *camera run-thru*—this is time when the director goes into the booth and calls the shots as if the show were actually being taped. If there were confusion about which camera was to be used, we might rehearse it once or twice until everyone understood. While segments may seem to be spontaneous, they are, in fact, well-rehearsed. This prevents a sloppy production.

Another segment that might have to be rehearsed would be one with an expert who has to use a cue card that matches the Chyron. Catching on to the terminology? It is better for a guest to become comfortable with cue cards, and for the booth to synchronize the Chyrons with the speed of the guest's speech, *before* the taping rather than *during* it. Remember, the more stop downs, the farther behind the production gets, which could result in lunch penalties. Besides, there were another two hours of taping after the first taping ended.

It was now about forty-five minutes until air. The host retired to his dressing room for makeup, hair, wardrobe, and lunch, which was served in the green room—I've never seen one that was actually painted green. Lunch was served, and we all attempted to keep the atmosphere as casual as possible to relax the guests for a broadcast that would be seen by millions.

In just a few minutes, the host would be introduced to the audience, and the crew and talent would take their places onstage, backstage, in the control room, tape room, audio and lighting rooms, and master control. It was show time!

In the meantime, the audience that had been waiting in line for up to two hours was admitted to the studio. The warm-up guy, hired to keep the audience entertained and to instruct them how and when to applaud, greeted them. Tapings can get tiresome because of long delays, and it is up to the warm-up guy to keep the audience fresh. There is always an inevitable delay because of a technical problem or because a guest is late.

My most remarkable example of a late-arriving performer was Lana Turner. Since many of her elderly fans had attended the taping just to see her, there was electricity in the studio. During the commercials between segments, I was called backstage to the studio phone to listen to Ms. Turner's segment producer, who was in a state of panic. Known for her agoraphobia, Ms. Turner had locked herself in the bathroom of her condo in Century City and refused to come out. I asked to speak with her, but she wouldn't open the door. Finally, as I completed taping all other elements in the show, I received word that Ms. Turner had finally emerged from the bathroom and was on her way.

"How long will it take her to get ready?" I asked. "Two hours." "Two hours?" Knowing that my warm-up comic had two hours to kill, I walked to the stage and asked to speak with him. "Marc, Lana is running a little late. You'll have to tread water for a while." Used to delays, Marc said, "Fine. How long?" "Two hours." "Two hours?" We needed the audience to give Lana Turner a standing ovation appropriate to a classic film star, so I joined Marc to keep the audience entertained—we told jokes, bantered, interviewed audience members, played games, and even introduced staff members. Amazingly, not one audience member left, and Lana Turner made her triumphant entrance to thunderous applause and a standing ovation! It looked so easy when I saw the final tape!

Post-Production Editing

It might seem that the completion of a studio taping would mean that all my concerns for an episode were at an end—that, as show runner, whether the broadcast was good or bad, I could put it all behind me and move on to the next show. The fact is that a show runner is also responsible for the next step in production—all editing aspects of the show, from the field or *remote pieces* (those pieces taped on location) to the completion and approval of the *final cut*, the last edit with all refinements that will become the air show or the program as it will be broadcast.

The phrase "I'll fix it in post" is a combination inside joke, industry cliché, or inexcusable response for something that should have been perfect before leaving the studio. But it is also a remarkable hi-tech, face-saving tool for which I have often been most grateful.

On literally hundreds of occasions, a host, knowing that a program is to be edited, has ignored the time signals. Usually the host had an agenda for an interview and was determined to complete that agenda without devoting hours to deciding how to reduce an eleven-minute segment to seven minutes while maintaining a cohesive whole. On a poorly edited

HOUR MAGAZINE RUN-DOWN
SHOW #640AA
VTR: 5/11-4:00 P.M.
AIR: 7/5

SEGMENT	ACTION	PROPS	AREA	SEGMENT TIME	TRT (TOTAL RUNNING TIME)
1	GARY INTROS SHOW W/VTPB (VIDEO-TAPE PLAYBACK)		DEN	:40	
	OPENING ANIMATION			:22	
	(CUE APPLAUSE)				
	GARY INTROS DEBBI MORGAN		HB (HOME BASE)	:20	
	DEBBI ENTERS FROM FRENCH DOORS, GOES TO HB				
	MUSIC CUE: THEME FROM *ALL MY CHILDREN* **CUE APPLAUSE**				
	DEBBI MORGAN INTERVIEW	2 PIX OF CHILDREN		7:00	
	MATTE Debbi Morgan *All My Children*				
	BUMPER OUT OF SEGMENT 1				
	TEXT: ADOPTED CHILD RETURNED TO BIOLOGICAL MOTHER MUSIC: MUSIC PACKAGE-SERIOUS VIDEO: NEWSPAPER HEADLINE			:12 SEG TIME 8:34	8:34

	COMM'L #1 (COMMERCIAL)			2:02	10:36

SEGMENT	ACTION	PROPS	AREA	SEGMENT TIME	TRT (TOTAL RUNNING TIME)
2	BUMPER INTO SEGMENT 2				
	VIDEO: ANIMATED LOGO #1			:10	
	MUSIC: MUSIC PACKAGE-SERIOUS				
	NOTE: NO APPLAUSE THROUGHOUT SEGMENT				
	GARY INTROS PIECE		HB	:30	
	BONNIE STRAUSS INTERVIEWS BIOLOGICAL MOTHER & ATTORNEY		DEN	8:00	

SEGMENT	ACTION	PROPS	AREA	SEGMENT TIME	TRT
	MATTE **Bonnie Strauss** Co-Host Patty Cochrane Biological Mother Regains Custody Helen Ramirez Attorney				
	BUMPER OUT OF SEGMENT 2				
	VIDEO: LIZ SMITH VTR MUSIC: "THAT'S ENTERTAINMENT," TEXT: CELEBRITY LIFE WITH LIZ			:12 SEG TIME 8:40	19:28
	COMM'L #2			2:02	21:30
3	BUMPER INTO SEGMENT 3				
	VIDEO: LIZ SMITH VTPB MUSIC: MUSIC PACKAGE-LIGHT			:12	
	GARY INTROS LIZ SMITH		VIDEO ROOM	:20	
	LIZ SMITH VTPB			4:18	
	MATTE Liz Smith Celebrity Reporter				
	GARY OUTRO & TEASE SEGMENT 4		VIDEO ROOM	:20	
	BUMPER OUT OF SEGMENT 3				
	TEXT: SINGLE AFTER 50 MUSIC: "ALONE AGAIN NATURALLY" VIDEO: PHOTO OF SINGLE WOMEN			:12 SEG TIME: 5:30	26:40
	COMM'L #3			2:02	28:54
4	BUMPER INTO SEGMENT 4				
	VIDEO: ANIMATED LOGO #5 MUSIC: PACKAGE-MODERATE			:12	
	GARY INTROS GUESTS		DEN	7:30	
	(PRE-SET)				
	MATTE Dr. Karen Fritts Psychologist Marilee Davis Single After 50				

SEGMENT	ACTION	PROPS	AREA	SEGMENT TIME	TRT
	BUMPER OUT OF SEGMENT 4				36:38
	TEXT: DO MEN HAVE PMS? VIDEO: GROUP PHOTO OF MEN MUSIC: "BEEN A BAD DAY"			:12 SEG TIME 7:54	

	COMM'L #4			2:02	38:40

SEGMENT	ACTION	PROPS	AREA	SEGMENT TIME	TRT
	BUMPER INTO SEGMENT 5 VIDEO: ANIMATED LOGO #3 MUSIC: PACKAGE-MODERATE			:12	
5	GARY INTERVIEWS MEN FROM AUDIENCE ABOUT PMS	RF MIC (HAND MIC)	AUDIENCE	1:40	
	GARY INTROS TAPE			:20	
	MALE PMS CLINIC VTPB			5:07	
	MATTE Dr. Joseph Futuci Urologist Tom Clifton Male PMS				
	GARY OUTRO & TEASES SEGMENT 6			:25	
	BUMPER OUT OF SEGMENT 5				
	TEXT: TONI'S TENDER TENDERLOINS **VIDEO: LIVE SHOT OF TONI COOKING** MUSIC: "LOVE WILL KEEP US TOGETHER"		DEMO	:12 SEG TIME 5:55	46:36

	COMM'L #5			2:02	48:38

SEGMENT	ACTION	PROPS	AREA	SEGMENT TIME	TRT
6	BUMPER INTO SEGMENT 6			:12	
	MUSIC-"LOVE WILL KEEP US TOGETHER" VIDEO-ANIMATED LOGO #7				
	GARY INTROS TONI TENNILLE		DEMO	:20	
	TONI STEPS INTO FRAME				
	(CUE APPLAUSE)	ROLL TABLE PROPS HAS LIST OF INGREDIENTS		6:00	
	MATTE Toni Tennille				
	BUMPER OUT OF SEGMENT 6				

SEGMENT	ACTION	PROPS	AREA	SEGMENT TIME	TRT
	TEXT: LET'S TASTE! VIDEO: KEEP ACTION GOING W/VIDEO MUSIC-PACKAGE-LIGHT			:12 SEG TIME 6:32	55:10

SEGMENT	ACTION	PROPS	AREA	SEGMENT TIME	TRT
	COMM'L #6			2:02	57:12

SEGMENT	ACTION	PROPS	AREA	SEGMENT TIME	TRT
7	BUMPER INTO SEGMENT 7			:12	
	VIDEO-ANIMATED LOGO #8				
	MUSIC-PACKAGE-LIGHT				
	GARY TASTES DISH AND THANKS TONI **(CUE APPLAUSE)**		DEMO	1:00	
	BYE & CREDITS			21 SEG TIME 1:33	58:45

program, even viewers can observe a "jump" in both video and audio, making them aware that the interview they are watching is not live, but the result of tampering. Viewers often resent this fact, thinking they have been deprived of content they would have liked to see.

More often than not, though, the material that has been "chopped" is extraneous and not worth the effort or expense. Of course, I would chastise, cajole, tease—in short, do everything in my power to force talent to remain within the confines of the time allotted to a particular segment. When these techniques proved to be unsuccessful, I would begin to give a *short count*—time signals that demonstrate less time than actually exists until commercial. Another technique I employed was to hold up a cue card that said, "Breath between questions." That was my shorthand with the host that the palaver between host and guest was going to be cut, and I wanted "the edit" to be a clean one. You can see how the relationship between a show runner and talent is like any other personal relationship—there are going to be differences, but if there is a strong bond between you, you can weather those bad moments. Can you imagine how a host would react to a cue card like that if our basic relationship were stormy? That's the time when a show runner leaves "to pursue other career opportunities."

When it became obvious during the taping that a segment would need a "cure" in post-production, I would tell the director I needed as many *cutaways* or *"listening shots,"* in which a person just reacts to what someone else is supposedly saying, and *long shots* from the studio audience to separate an answer from the next question. These shots would be inserted wherever necessary. Then I would talk down all elements with the associate director to determine whether we needed to do a pickup of a particular question and answer. Of course, it was always delicate to hop onto the set just after we faded to black to tell the host and/or guest that something was awry. It was amazing how a self-confident person could become totally insecure because a portion of the interview had to be retaped. I learned a great deal about how to deal with a variety of egos—who needed coddling, who responded best to "straight talk," and who would object the most.

In most situations, everyone agreed to follow my requests. Yet as I knew "when to hold 'em," I also had to know when to "fold 'em" because if the resistance I encountered was too great, any retaping would only result in worse results. On those occasions I would ask the AD to send his *first cut*—the first edit of any tape—of the segment to my office, and we would try to make everyone look his/her best.

Field Pieces

Nearly every studio-based show has at least one field segment per episode—and often more, depending upon the nature and budget of the series. I would meet with the head of the division to approve the selection of material in a field-produced segment and view the first cut as well as all subsequent cuts. A great deal of my time was spent viewing edited video.

With a field piece that had begun from a concept, it was both creative and satisfying to watch the story take shape, from the acceptance of the basic story through the development of the elements to be shot on location and the submission of a *shot sheet*—the camera shots that the field producer hoped to tape for the segment. Once the segment was put on tape, it would usually be edited before the show runner viewed the first cut. Typically, there was too little time for me to view all the *raw footage*—unedited footage—for every piece.

After the first cut, a meeting would be held or notes sent about every aspect of the piece: the main idea of the story, the length of the story, the selection of music, the quality of the script that tells the story and bridges the video, and the effectiveness of the *sound bites*—what individuals say in the segment (also known as *SOT*, sound on tape). Are the SOT too long, too short, or just right? Do they enhance and maximize the dramatic effect of the piece? Have the *VOs*—voice-overs by the talent—been read with the appropriate attitude and enough energy?

Since only one camera is used in the field, the camera is usually focused on the person or people being interviewed, with *reverses*—pointing the camera back toward the interviewer, giving the impression that more than one camera is being used and the illusion that the answer directly follows the question. If I were unhappy after analyzing everything, I had to decide if I would return to the raw footage, re-conceptualize the edit, do a *kill* (decide not to run the piece at all, sometimes known as *eating it*), or ask for a re-shoot if possible—if all the elements were not there. The field producers who didn't deliver were replaced. Because of the costs, poor results were unacceptable.

Sample Segment

Let me offer a clear example of the elements involved in the development, shooting, and editing of a field piece. This piece was to be for the 1990s version of *Mickey Mouse Club*. Because we had a target audience of pre-teens, we devoted about a third of each Friday's episode to honoring two special young people by awarding them a statuette suitably named The Mickey. One segment would feature a live performer, such as a singer, dancer, or musician. This segment was taped in the studio. The second segment was a field piece about someone whose achievements were praiseworthy.

A particularly memorable *package*—a self-contained field piece—was about Travis, a ten-year-old boy who, despite a muscle-wasting disease, refused to allow his disability to interfere with his quality of life. He enjoyed reading, going to the library, eating at McDonald's—and especially playing with his golden lab, who assisted him with his every move. The dog would position himself to assist Travis, lying down to give Travis a push-off point or rising up on his back legs at the library counter to return a book. The two even went in the backyard sliding pond together. At the same time, Travis had a wonderful relationship with his mother, who was supportive of Travis's living as normal a life as possible.

After looking at the story, we had to make choices about what we wanted to tell. We could have honored Travis by showing him coping with life's daily struggles, emphasized his mother's instilling confidence in a severely disabled son, or focused on the warm relationship between a son and mother that was all the more poignant because of the support they gave each other. However, we knew *before* we shot the piece that we wanted to tell the story of the relationship between the boy and his dog. They loved each other and each thrived on the bond between them.

After watching the opening montage, it was obvious that we had an outstanding story about a young boy whose best friend was a canine, and a canine whose love was non-judgmental and unconditional. The dog licked the boy's ice-cream cone; they played Frisbee together; the two lay intertwined when they took naps. The mother was quoted, but she was properly secondary to the piece. Besides receiving a huge outpouring of positive responses from our viewers, we were awarded a Media Access Award for the positive depiction of the disabled.

Field Production Staffing

I am purposely being a bit vague about the personnel involved in a field unit because it varies. While a studio staff must have its researchers, talent coordinators, and segment/episode producers, a field production staff can consist simply of one producer who uses freelancers to a group of producers, directors, and even editors who are part of the staff on a full-time basis. The number of possible staff scenarios is enormous. For example, studio staff might supply stories for remote segments—or the field unit may be a separate department on the show that serves just its own needs. While producers might shoot pieces anywhere in the world, they often send their raw footage to the city in which production takes place. I have supervised shows in which the editors also serve as post-production producers, creating their entire final package. Just how field production is supplied depends on the number of pieces required each week, the budget, and the show runner's decision as to what constitutes optimal efficiency.

The Hot Edit

In this era of a hundred or so cable networks, and the resulting low budgets, there is often *absolutely no budget for editing.* That means the show you complete in the studio is the exact show that will appear on air. This even includes credits and logos with timing down to the exact second—it's as though it were a live show. However, when a show is not actually live, but on tape, there is a solution to your not having a budget for editing. The answer is the hot edit—rolling back the tape and re-shooting the portion containing the error so that it exactly matches the footage and mood that preceded it. No easy task!

With a staff of four, including me, I did a syndicated show called *Body by Jake*, featuring fitness trainer Jake Steinfeld. Because *Body by Jake* had a small number of viewers—those who were awake when the show aired between 4:00 A.M.–6:00 A.M., it generated low advertising revenue. This meant there was an incredibly low budget that made the production barely possible. As a result, I had to tape twelve half-hour shows every weekend—six on Saturday and six on Sunday. Whenever Jake would stumble on words or ask an inappropriate question, or if the director called for the wrong shot, I stopped taping immediately to do a "hot edit." This meant rolling back the tape to the sentence just before the error. Then the tape would be *played to the floor*—appear on the monitors in the studio—and the tape operator would freeze the picture. Jake had to move into the *exact* same spot, with his body in *exactly* the same position. The TD would fade from the previous tape to the live shot to make sure it was an exact match. Then we would retape the problem lines. Each error made another hot edit necessary, thereby eating into valuable time during a six-show day. By the way, since every dollar was significant for this show, I had to watch the clock nervously, because the budget allowed for absolutely no overtime.

The only alternative to the hot edit is to retape the entire segment; in fact, sometimes it is quicker to do that if you're within the first minute or two of the segment. The downside of this technique is that, as a host and guest repeat moments, energy and spontaneity often flag, resulting in lesser performances. As show runner, I always had to make a judgment call—sometimes right and sometimes wrong—about whether to take the time for a hot edit or just begin again.

It's Not Even Over When It's Over

As you can see, the responsibilities of the show runner begin with the conception of each episode and are not completed until the final tape is approved for air. Even then his job is not over, because viewers have both positive and negative reactions to everything that is seen. Therefore, the final edited tape often results in complaints by viewers. They call the production office or, worse, the local station airing the program. If the viewers are not happy, the stations are not happy—and guess who has to answer for everything that is aired?

The twists and turns are constant, and the amount of time necessary to do a good job is infinite. When the phone rings—at the office during the day and at home any hour of the night—the call could be about a show in the planning stages, one about to be taped, another in post-production, or one being reacted to by the public. It never gets dull!

FLOOR PRODUCING A SEASON OF SHOWS

FLOOR PRODUCING: IT'S MAGIC TIME!

Based on all the old movies about putting a show on Broadway, one would think that, once all the preparation and rehearsals were completed, the producer or show runner could sit back, watch the show, and hope for the best. Nothing could be further from the truth. A potentially outstanding episode can fizzle if the show runner doesn't take charge to make sure that everyone, from the talent to the staff, to the director and technical crew, is clicking. Or a seemingly mediocre show can become excellent if the show runner makes on-the-spot, creative decisions that allow the show to take fire. These on-air decisions are the true test of a show runner's grace under pressure.

I rarely wore a headset during *Hour Magazine* tapings to avoid struggling to hear the content being taped. Because of all the conversations between the director and technical people on headset, my concentration could become diverted. I preferred, instead, to use "hotline" phones located on each side of the stage to connect me directly to the booth. The hotline would be answered by the ubiquitous 1st/Booth PA, who would pass my note to the associate director (AD) for editing, or to the director. At other times, I wished to speak directly to the director because I felt a series of shots had been sloppy or had not captured a moment. Using this private line ensured that our conversation would not be overheard and embarrass the director. At other times, I had to revise times for the remaining segments with the PA or make editing notes to give to the AD before he went into the editing room. I always carried at least a dozen large, blank cue cards, which were ready for me to scribble notes for the talent. These notes could include comments such as a follow-up question that had been missed.

I stood just a few feet in front of the talent(s), behind the guest(s), and within two feet of the camera shot. To a member of the audience, I probably looked like part of the show. Standing next to me would be the segment/episode producer, so we could confer at a moment's notice. If we agreed to make a change, I wrote the change on a cue card and held it up for the talent.

Every talent is comfortable with a different amount of information and text, and the job of the show runner is to make sure that the talent is not hampered by too much or too little material. For example, Regis Philbin works with just a few index cards for notes, although he has been briefed about areas of conversation. He does not want a producer controlling what he says or does on air. During the many years that I worked with Gary Collins as the host of *Hour Magazine*, we both realized he was at his best if he did not have to improvise. Therefore, he read all introductions from the copy on the TelePrompTer and relied on one large cue card just out of camera range. On the cue card were all the questions prepared by the segment/episode producer, as well as any additional questions Gary had requested. In this way, Gary would have everything he needed, whether he was facing the camera or the card. It was always advantageous to write the name of the guest at the top of the cue card, so that Dr. Goldsmith did not inadvertently become Dr. Goldstein.

SOMETIMES THERE ARE HICCUPS

During the years I worked with Gary, as with every host with whom I have ever worked, I used floor producing to protect him when he would inadvertently say something inappropriate. Let me give you a couple of examples.

We were doing a story about a recruit who had drowned under mysterious circumstances during basic training at Paris Island. The family was angry that the government had not investigated the drowning because they strongly believed foul play was involved. Gary's follow-up question was, "Where is the investigation now. Dead in the water, so to speak?" The question could not be aired that way because it would have made Gary seem insensitive to the tragic death of the family's son. Sure, I could have spoken up immediately, asking Gary to take a brief pause to allow for the edit, and then have him re-ask the question. However, the parents were understandably emotional and interruption of the interview would have spoiled the effect.

Instead, I lifted my hotline phone to tell the 1st/Booth PA that we would do a pickup, redoing a section after it is completed. The 1st/ Booth PA told the director, who instructed the stage manager not to allow anyone to move when Gary ended the interview, and *threw to commercial*—preview what is coming up in the next segment and break for commercial. At that point, I took Gary aside to discuss the situation privately. It is always more appropriate to isolate the talent in a situation like this to avoid embarrassment. The show runner must always take responsibility for making sure that the talent is at his best so he is relaxed and comfortable throughout the taping. Otherwise, viewers will be aware that the host is having an off day. I tried to make it appear that there were no off days for Gary.

During the pickup, we would take a *one-shot*—only one person on camera—of Gary asking a question that would be inserted into the edited tape. In addition, we would tape listening shots, in which a person just reacts to what someone else is supposedly saying, of both Gary and each of the guests. Therefore, when the segment was edited, we could go to any of the above to make a smooth edit. For a show that uses audience shots, pickups can also include listening shots of individuals or groups in the audience. If the viewer can't tell that there has been an edit because of a sudden jump, the pickups have been successful.

In another instance, Gary was interviewing a father from Alaska whose twelve-year-old son had rescued him when he fell through an ice-covered lake and nearly froze and drowned. It was one of our recurring "Great American Hero" sequences that honored regular people who had acted in remarkable or heroic manners. The payoff to the segment, which, of course, was prearranged, was Duke, the father, presenting Gary with a frozen fish brought from Alaska. I mean this fish was frozen solid! Gary's remark was, "Hey Duke, this could have been you!" Everyone laughed, even Duke, but the remark had to go because it changed the mood to one of great levity. I stopped tape. I had to stop tape because if there were a pickup at the end, the moods might not match. I took Gary aside to explain why we had to retape, beginning with the presentation of the frozen fish.

One last example was with a host, who will remain nameless, for a program that, thank goodness, did not have a studio audience. The program was for a magazine show about alternative healing, relaxation, and sports, and the setting was an exterior and interior facsimile of a five-star hotel. I have told the following story to many people, none of whom has ever believed that the host fought me about retaping his remarks. The segment was about the use of candles to set a mood, mostly for romance. As the guest presented a variety of candles and aromas, the male host told her that he lit candles when he took a bath with his then-seven-year-old daughter, whose custody he shared with his ex-wife. He said he often prepared a bath for the two of them with candles, because it helped to relax the child.

I happened to be in the booth at that moment. All jaws dropped; every eye turned to me. I asked to have tape stopped immediately, knowing the implications of his story, and headed at top speed for the stage. By the time I got there, the 1st stage manager had already stopped the segment. However, instead of being grateful I was protecting him, the host was irate. When I went over to speak with him he asked, "What was wrong?" I said, "Let's talk privately." When I got him to the side and told him that it would be better if he did not tell the story about bathing in candlelight with his daughter, he said loudly and angrily, "Hey, I ain't no perv." I said that no one was accusing him of being one—discretion is important in these situations. Although he insisted that his conduct was appropriate, I insisted that we retape *without* the story. He agreed reluctantly.

In that case, I was prepared to go to the mat in order to win that battle. Not only was his reputation at stake—even though he was too dense to realize it—but mine was as well. I could not allow such a statement on-air on moral grounds. What the host did with his daughter was not my business—although I certainly question the reasons for and advisability of such an activity—but the show that appeared with my name attached to it was my responsibility. We began the segment from *the top*—the time coming out of commercial—so that it could begin fresh.

PREPPING FOR EDIT

Another common problem with talent during a show is they become so engrossed in the content of the segment they go over the allotted time given on the rundown. They know we edit the show and, therefore, feel they can take an additional minute, or two, or even three to complete their agendas for the interview. Sometimes no amount of waving *bye-bye* from me, or the twist of a closed fist from the stage manager to wrap it —finish up—deterred a determined host from his mission. As a result, when the interview was finished we had to do a cutaway for each of the participants in the segment. Therefore, as we edited out content, we could go to a shot of the host listening to the guest, or vice versa, until we got to the section where we wished to continue. When doing cutaways, no one is allowed to mutter a single sound, or else there will be *lip flap*—movement of the lips with no sound being heard.

As I watched a segment being taped, I was always playing the edit in my head, because I knew even then what I wanted to keep and what I wanted to purge. Often I would extend a segment by one to three minutes because I had heard a section that was dull, ineffective, or irrelevant, which I knew would have to be edited out. This editing information would be phoned to the 1st/Booth PA, so that everyone knew we were *holding*—continuing with the interview in progress— and which portion I intended to remove. Additionally, if an important question had not received the response I expected, I would ask the host and guest to "pick up" just that portion of the interview. This was after I had explained to them what I felt had been missed in the initial taping. In that way, I got the interview I believed was most effective.

While watching and listening to the host and guest(s), I was also keeping an eye on a video monitor, so I could see the shots that the director was selecting at each moment. On a lower-budget show, not every camera could be an iso and, even if there were several, I could not be sure they captured the exact shot that I needed. In addition, a director sometimes got so involved in the action that key moments were missed because he chose a *long shot* (one taken from a distance) or *medium shot* (one taken from the chest up) when a *CU* (close-up) or *ECU* (extreme close-up) would have better captured the moment.

The show runner must watch both the floorshow as well as the monitor in order to compare what is actually happening with the director's choices. Talk about multi-tasking!

BUT WAIT, THERE'S MORE!

While all this was happening, members of my staff were continually consulting with me about changes, additions, or dropouts, and the 2nd stage manager—through the 1st stage manager—kept me informed about problems, such as a guest not arriving on time.

Since the studio audience is part of any show, I also had to work with the warm-up person and the audience itself. For example, if we were dealing with a serious subject, such as incest, I would not want audience applause to accompany or end the segment. I had already been introduced to the audience, so they knew that I ran the show. So I instructed the warm-up man, who relayed to the audience what was needed.

Typically the warm-up people were comedians at the beginning of their careers. At night they would play The Comedy Store and The Improv, and this union job of warming up an audience helped pay the rent while they were pursuing stardom. I remember one warm-up man, a brash young guy who was "striking out" with the older people in the audience at *Hour Magazine*. Backstage, he kept apologizing profusely because he needed the money and was afraid we'd never use him again. His name was Jerry Seinfeld.

Usually a one-hour broadcast took about two hours to tape because of all the stop downs, pickups, cutaways, and resolution of an assortment of problems. Finally, though, it would be over. Just when most people would be ready to crawl into bed to take a nap, I had to grab my script book and head back upstairs to get ready for the second show. After all, taping was just two hours away!

6

MICKEY MOUSE CLUB

REPACKAGING A FAILED PILOT

I would never have believed during my formative years, when I watched nearly *everything* on television, that I would one day produce the one show that was certainly a classic of my childhood—*Mickey Mouse Club*. As children we would sing, "Who's the leader of the club that's made for you and me? M-I-C-K-E-Y M-O-U-S-E," and "See you real soon...Why? Because we like you." Now skip forward nearly thirty-five years—suddenly I was the executive producer of the *revival* of *Mickey Mouse Club*, with the mission of making a dated classic viable for a hip 1990s audience. Talk about "mission impossible!"

My adventure began between seasons of *Body by Jake*, not the most gratifying show to produce, with its staff of three besides me, and a budget in which an extra pair of sneakers could throw us over. So my antennae were out for a more challenging situation. But I should have remembered the old adage "be careful what you wish for," because challenge is exactly I got. One morning I was thumbing through my new issue of *TV Guide*—just as I had every week since the 1950s—when I noticed a special report about a "Disney disaster."

Apparently, a disastrous pilot had been shot to revive the classic *Mickey Mouse Club* series: It had cost the studio a staggering $5 million. The executive producer had been fired, and a national search had been started to find that special individual who could save this classic Disney franchise. As I read the article, I chuckled, thinking, "No way would I get involved in something like this. It's a no-win situation." The essence of the old show could not be recaptured for an MTV-savvy group of young people.

It was one of those truth-can-be-more-unbelievable-than-fiction situations when the phone rang about an hour later. The Disney Channel was calling. The executive on the phone said management had become aware of my work and was interested in interviewing me for executive producer of *Mickey Mouse Club*. Although I sounded calm and restrained on the phone, my jaw had dropped. I wanted to yell out, "I just read about this turkey, and can't believe that your national search has resulted in calling *me*!"

Despite protesting that I would never even consider such a series, I found myself thanking them for calling, and saying I would certainly be willing to meet. "How about next Tuesday," I volunteered? The executive countered, "How about this afternoon?" I heard myself say, "Sure," and a few hours later I was being interviewed by a group of Disney executives for a job of tremendous importance to the reputation of the Disney legacy.

After being handed a copy of the pilot, I was given a two-part assignment for the following twenty-four hours: analyze what was wrong with the pilot and be prepared to discuss how I would transform it into a hit. Cinch! All evening and the following morning I watched the show, took copious notes, and envisioned how to make the show work. Although this was a daunting task, it did supply a fresh source of the adrenaline that I thrived on.

At the meeting the next day, I apparently wowed them with my evaluations since they said I had "hit everything on the head." My suggestions were met with smiles and, by the end of the meeting, nearly every Disney executive had entered the room to shoot more questions at me. They wanted to know about my comedy-writing experience, producing experience, educational background and teaching experience, ability to withstand stress, availability to work in Orlando,

Florida, and dozens of other questions, many of which I could not see as relevant *at that time!* The reasons became perfectly clear, though, within the first few weeks after I began work. What I will never forget, though, was the final line of the interview, uttered by the leading executive—it still makes me shudder. It was, "You will have four weeks to make this show work. If you succeed, you will be a Disney hero. If you don't, you will never work for Disney again."

During the next two days, I fantasized about having success with a program most people agreed was hopeless, while my agent negotiated the contract. Once the terms were agreed upon, one loophole remained. I was required to fly to Orlando, along with the potential head writer and reality segment producer, to be "studied" for seventy-two hours! What did that mean? Television is a strange business filled with unusual requests, so I agreed to be studied. If I passed the test, I would have ten days to get ready to move to Orlando; if I failed, the contract would be null and void.

Never did they state the purpose of such study. For three days, three of us, along with the two major Disney executives, met for breakfast at The Grand Floridian hotel, then marched to a car that took us to the not-yet-completed Disney-MGM Studios and Theme Park. For about ten hours each day we talked—and talked—and talked about the show, the two executives continually glancing at each other. Then we talked some more at dinner. At breakfast on the third day, the top executive privately asked me to take the head writer and relax while he had a word with the man who was in line to be the reality producer. We never saw him again! I was told later that candidate had packed his bags and took the next plane out of there.

My position confirmed, I spent the next ten days astounded—well, perhaps panicked—by the enormity of the task ahead. I packed up my life, met with Los Angeles writers and potential staff members, went to New York, and interviewed still others. Time was short, and I was going to need many more people than were on board for the pilot, as well as replacements for those who did not have the talents I needed.

WHO'S THE LEADER OF THE CLUB?

By the time I arrived in Orlando, many of the new hires were checking in. I shook what felt like thousands of hands of those I would be supervising for this production. We started with about a dozen Mouseketeers, who eventually became twenty-four (you know how mice proliferate), two adult hosts, a staff of 152 people, plus dozens of crewmembers. In addition, each child had at least one parent in town, and there was a school on the lot with eight teachers and an educational program that met the standards of the state of Florida. I was the principal of the school, which was why they were so interested in my educational and teaching background. Therefore, not only did I have to worry about the quality of the show, I had to be concerned about why Albert was having problems with science! The cost of the production was a mind-boggling *$1 million a week!* There would be musical numbers with Broadway-quality sets, costumes, and choreography; reality segments; entertaining educational material; games; comedy sketches and *blackouts*—short sketches, usually running less than a minute that parody commercials and movies; musical guest stars; and MTV-quality music videos.

One of my comments when I saw the pilot was it was unclear who the target audience demographic was. As a result, some of the material seemed to be infantile for a preteen audience, while other elements seemed too sophisticated for a younger audience. In television, as it is with the rest of industry, one of the most effective ways to find out how people feel about a product is to conduct focus groups. During focus groups in television, the leading creative people sit behind a two-way mirror, while a genial host shows pieces of videotape. The viewers might be housewives between the ages of forty-five and fifty-four, black teen males, Asian women between twenty-five and thirty-four, or any other specific audience demographic. By watching and listening to a focus group view a piece of the show on a screen, the creative people get a better idea of who is attracted to the show and why.

With *Mickey Mouse Club*, we had a major problem. On three separate occasions, I flew to Atlanta, along with producer Margie Friedman, head writer Alan Silberberg, and one to two Disney executives, to watch the reactions of little boys (five to seven), little girls (five to seven), older boys (eight to thirteen), and older girls (eight to thirteen). *All of them* said that they would definitely not watch the show. Why? No matter their age, the reason was the same—"Mickey Mouse is for babies."

This strongly negative reaction produced a chill down my spine. Mickey Mouse had been an icon of the Disney Company for sixty-five years. How could I change his image...and if I did, how would Michael Eisner (then-President and CEO) and the rest of the Disney brass feel about it?

Through the discussion with the focus group host, I learned something that made sense, but about which I was totally unaware: Every age group of children wants to *play up*—watch what older children watch. Therefore, if I were to set my sites at appealing to children thirteen and older, I would get children up to that age, even if the thirteen-year-olds themselves did not watch.

First of all, we decided the mouse ears had to go! All children found them unhip and would not want to be caught watching a program featuring performers wearing ears. This would incur ridicule among their peers. In addition, the music had to have an edge to it comparable to that on MTV. Rather than using simple, happy tunes with simple singing and dancing, the musical numbers would be concept-driven. For example, if we were to do James Brown's hit "I Feel Good," it would not be sung by a precious darling staring into the camera and belting out the song. Instead, we would create an action- and dance-driven story, such as one in which a conceited, handsome young man walks through a schoolyard set, being pursued by females. He then sings the song with attitude, while several females, serving as chorus and doing "hip hop" dancing, pursue him. Perhaps, by the end of the number, an even more attractive young man would come along, and the girls would all turn to him. When the song and story end, the new guy is the hero and the original male is completely crushed. The moral is that no one is irreplaceable. We all like to watch someone who's cocky get his just desserts. Entertainment with a message!

It was also agreed that comedy sketches had to have an edge that was similar to those on *Saturday Night Live*. The writers would search for various characters who would be *refillable*—performed again and again—under different circumstances. In that way, it would mirror the longtime NBC show, which over the years has included everything from John Belushi's "Samurai Warrior" to Dana Carvey's "Church Lady," to

Eddie Murphy's "Mr. Robinson's Neighborhood." We would have quick blackouts as well as full sketches with the most popular characters.

Based on the focus groups, we realized that our target audience was predominantly female. Boys were more interested in action series and cartoons, and didn't care to watch singing and dancing. Therefore, we maximized the sex appeal of the male cast, while providing attractive young ladies to entice male viewers to watch.

Mickey himself needed updating, and even Disney was willing to cooperate since the executives were aware of the erosion of enthusiasm for the corporate rodent. We consulted with a number of designers to determine how to repackage Mickey to attract older children. When we were given illustrations of Mickey in a striped rugby shirt, everything clicked. Mickey's face was changed to an older, campier image while retaining something of the familiar Disney icon. Mickey no longer resembled the mouse with which every three-year-old had had her picture taken.

Add to this updated image a rap version of the *Mickey Mouse Club* theme, and we had the beginnings of a show that would appeal to pre-teens. If preteens watched, every child up to that age would watch. We knew it would also be important to show audience members who reflected that older demographic. When we began taping the show, all young children—those under ten—were placed in the studio audience where they would not be seen on camera. The older teen and preteen kids were seated up front and pre-selected to be shown throughout the program.

I returned to Orlando with my associates to face the challenge of trying to make this thirty-five-year-old show new and hip while not offending parents and grandparents to whom the original show was a classic. I realized I would have a long and difficult road ahead.

KEEPING TO THE SCHEDULE

I faced my work in Orlando as the biggest challenge of my career. During my years as show runner for non-fiction television shows such as *Hour Magazine*, our regimented schedule did not vary from week to week. Not so with *Mickey Mouse Club*! Predictability was just not possible with twenty-four Mouseketeers and enough aggressive stage mothers to make *Gypsy's* Mama Rose seem like a shrinking violet.

There were also two adult hosts, a staff of 152 people, and dozens of crew personnel, all controlled by the people who ran "the happiest place on earth"—The Walt Disney Company. Rather than feeling like the executive producer, I felt more like the mayor of a small city.

MY SO-CALLED SCHEDULE

Since each day was different, with the only constant being the 4:00 P.M.–6:30 P.M. studio tapings every other week, it is impossible to tell exactly what happened on each day of the week. This, then, is a partial list of my activities for a week, with the biggest crisis at any particular moment receiving highest priority for my attention:

On any given day, I met with the writers to accept and reject sketch, blackout, and game-show concepts and suggest places where improvements were needed. Since I was also one of the writers for the show, we would all *improv*—make up dialogue as we went along—a comedy concept, with the head writer, six staff writers, and me throwing out jokes until the first draft of a sketch was created. After leaving a comedy meeting, I might have to read curricula submitted in each discipline by our eight onsite teachers since I served as principal of the school. In turn, I would report to a superintendent of schools, who flew from New York periodically to meet with the teachers, students, and me to ensure that we were following Florida state guidelines in each subject. No youngster was permitted to appear on stage without at least a C average. Therefore, if Brandy had a solo in a huge production number, I had to pray that she passed her history exam so she would qualify to tape. On one occasion, eleven-year-old Lindsey Alley, who had absolutely no stage fright, hid under my desk because of her math phobia. I crawled under my desk, and together we did her homework. This was not a typical show!

Other duties included meeting with my co-producer, Margie Friedman, to discuss the aspects of the *reality segments* of the show—which were on-location, non-fiction, magazine-type stories about young people who were contributing in a special way to society, or segments giving selected viewers an opportunity to spend a day with their favorite celebrities or exploring an occupation by having a viewer assist someone in that field. For example, one child wanted to be a veterinarian so, we documented her day working with an actual veterinarian. One young man wanted to be an entrepreneur and, to my amazement, Donald Trump allowed this young man to be his assistant for an entire day. This resulted in a wonderful piece, with Donald Trump as the perfect mentor and host.

Other meetings I had were with each of the other departments: the music department to work on concepts for musical numbers; the celebrity talent department to decide which top musical acts at $20,000 an appearance we should book; the budget and accounting departments to find out whether we had money to spend; the research department to hear about new story ideas and to decide which ones should be pursued; and the promotion department to plan contests and media appearances to improve visibility for the show. I visited the rehearsal halls to give notes to the heads of each department and brought notes from Disney in Burbank about Standards and Practices objections.

I was the first to review our *rough cuts*—first edits without finishing touches with which the show can be viewed before money is spent to prepare a complete, polished product. After Disney looked at the tape, I would have to defend and/or agree with the vice-president of production about sketches he did not find funny and felt should be scrapped, the editing choices made in musical numbers, and the order of the various elements of the show. This was a particularly difficult part of my job because I was not dealing with an executive who was experienced in television production. He had been an accountant for both Paramount and Disney before becoming a television executive.

In addition, I would meet with the Disney executive who was in Orlando, who had her own agenda about what the show should and should not be. It was whatever would give her the greatest glory and put her in line for promotion at the network. When this executive did not get her way, she would cry hysterically in front of staff, cast, and parents—truly an embarrassment.

The task I enjoyed least was listening to the sometimes violent complaints of a Mouseketeer parent, who believed that her child was far more talented than any other child or was being discriminated against by having the fewest songs, sketches, or introductions. There was even one parent who, when she couldn't convince me her daughter should be selected to sing a Mariah Carey hit, had the child chase a Disney executive down the street singing the song in full voice. As the executive began to run, so did the girl! On many occasions, I would receive calls at home and, if they were angry enough, during the middle of the night from irate parents ready to shriek at me about their child's not being given the opportunity to demonstrate her unique talents. The demands were often accompanied by threats of walking off the show and, in more than one case, they did—and the show went on. Just like any prime-time show that has a cast change, fans initially call and write letters asking what happened to the missing cast member. Then life continues. Those who walked off the show usually walked into permanent obscurity.

Despite the enormous amount of work involved in delivering five half-hour shows a week, we still had to produce them within a ten-hour day that allowed three hours of schooling for each child, rehearsals for all aspects of the show, and a taping in a too-small, poorly air-conditioned studio. In addition, the studio had to accommodate a studio audience of 200, mostly hormonal girls, who screamed at the sight of their favorite cast members.

GENERAL ORGANIZATION

With so many juvenile cast members and so many areas of activity, I had one staff member whose sole job was to track the location of every cast member at every moment of every day. This was done through color-coding—let's say we used yellow for Josh and green for Jennifer. If I wanted to know where Jennifer was at any particular moment, I could check the time and look for green to find out she was in school, for instance. She could have been in the dance rehearsal trailer, in the recording studio doing pre-recording, on location in the park shooting a comedy sketch, somewhere in Orlando shooting part of a music video, in a rehearsal hall practicing her introductions, in another rehearsal hall rehearsing a comedy sketch—and so on. I sometimes felt as if I were the general in a war, consulting to find out where each of my troops was stationed.

SO MUCH TO DO, SO LITTLE TIME

With so many departments contributing to *Mickey Mouse Club*, as well as a studio that was micro-managing every element and frame of the show, I realized that, while I could be the show runner, I could not control every moment of the show. There were just not enough hours in the day, not even if I worked 24/7. I could not tape the studio portions of the show every week because of the complexity of the production, as well as the limitations imposed on us by child labor laws and *SAG*—Screen Actors Guild. Therefore, I had to put my trust in my team of captains, which consisted of the reality producer, Margie Friedman; head writer, Alan Silberberg; executive in charge of production, Jean Wiegman; and the various people who headed the music division. If I had to be involved in one crisis to the extent it precluded my giving attention to other aspects of the show, these captains would take charge of their areas and report to me. Delegation of trust and responsibility to that extent was new for me, but was essential for the show's—and my—survival.

Realizing that we could not produce five shows in a five-day period, I asked Disney to allow me to tape five shows over a two-week period. As a result, we spent only one week out of two in the studio, taping everything that required a studio audience. In preparation for the studio week, we rehearsed all the musical numbers, sketch material, games, and hosting duties in rehearsal halls. In addition, by taping pieces of each show on location during these non-studio weeks, we had less material to be taped in front of a studio audience. That way, I could guarantee that a studio taping that began at 4:00 P.M. would end precisely at 6:30 P.M. when Disney pulled the plug. This was tense for me, since survival in the job depended upon my delivering each show on time and on budget. Yet my survival also depended upon adhering to legal and union rules. Even after all these years, I am still amazed I was able to delivery nearly 200 episodes on time and on budget.

For the first year, I was given leeway with regard to the 6:30 stop time. Disney was understanding about the impossibilities I faced partly because they were reveling in the fact that The Disney Channel had become a brand name because of this series. Then a frightening event occurred, threatening my reputation as well as that of the studio.

As a first anniversary special, we decided to unite the original cast from the 1950s, including the darling of the series, Annette Funicello, with the Mouseketeers of the 1990s. During the week of rehearsal, it was fascinating to watch the politics and resentments from thirty-five years earlier resurface. Annette, who had always been Walt Disney's favorite, was always the biggest star and was the one who had a career as a performer that outlasted the series. Of course, she was the one person we *had to have* in order to do the show. It would have meant nothing to have just Cubby, Darlene, and the others. Therefore, we had to pay Annette $20,000 for her appearance, which had to be completed before the others finished taping. The other original Mouseketeers received scale, which was about $500, plus expenses. Although each had animosities against some of the others, they seemed united in resenting Annette's preferential treatment.

On the evening Annette was to leave, we invited the press to watch the taping of the major musical number involving both old and new Mouseketeers. I stood backstage with my headset on—unlike *Hour Magazine,* I wore a headset so I could supervise such a complicated show from offstage—while I watched the action on the monitor. I couldn't believe my eyes when, in the middle of the number, a current Mouseketeer, Damon Pampolina, collapsed and fell flat on his face. Taping stopped; music stopped; all our hearts seemed to stop. Damon's mother ran out on the stage screaming, and I joined her, having never run that fast before. We called paramedics but, by the time they arrived, Damon was fine. It turned out Damon had not eaten all day, even though the entire studio adjacent to ours was being used as a catering hall, with a multitude of staff to feed cast, crew, staff, press, Disney—hundreds of people. Instead, he gobbled handfuls of M&Ms and swallowed a huge Coke, putting his sugar levels into shock.

The next day I was excoriated in *The Orlando Sentinel* as a child-abuser—someone who overworked children just for the sake of a television show. Other newspapers picked up on the story, and Disney was at risk of being the center of controversy. The last thing they needed was to be accused of abusing children. From that moment on, I had to practice everything exactly by the book. Now I had the extra pressure of completing my tapings not at 6:31 P.M., but by 6:30 P.M.

One would think that Disney executives would have lowered their standards of perfection because our time was now more limited. They did not. Instead, I received the usual perfectionist notes that could be accommodated only through an unlimited amount of time in the studio. For example, each musical number had to be taped four times by five cameras, with each camera being iso'd. That's a total of twenty views of the same musical number. We needed this in order to have enough choices for each and every moment of the one song. In the finished product, the first three words of the song might have been from camera 3 from the 1st take, the next four words might have been from Camera 2 from the 4th take, and the close-up of Tiffany might have come from Camera 1 in the 3rd take. Nevertheless, Disney would look at the *off-line edit*—editing process producing workprints not intended for air use but time coded into final form—and write me a note like: "14:21:13—Tiffany blinks. Use another shot, or reshoot entire number." This was an actual note—one of many just like it!

Because Disney was so insistent on approval rights for every aspect of the production, I made sure I had management's approval for everything, from the conception of every musical number and sketch through the *on-line edit*—master editing system using top-quality recorders for master tapes.

MUSICAL NUMBERS

On *Mickey Mouse Club,* there were two types of musical numbers: those videotaped in front of a studio audience and complex MTV-style music videos that had to be taped during the non-studio weeks. Some of the MTV-style numbers were shot on location while others employed *chromakey*—an effect that uses a blue or green screen against which any background can be placed. The process was the same for both types, although the music videos were produced and edited by David Seeger, who insisted on being called Mouseketeer Dave. Mouseketeer Dave came from New York City every two weeks in full 1955 *Mickey Mouse Club* regalia, including ears, to shoot video. He then edited the final video in his post-production studio in New York.

Before the editing process, though, songs had to be selected. The music department would submit a list of songs, and I would select the four to be produced each week—three in the studio and one as a music video. Then we had to get *licensing rights*. If the price was right, we proceeded to the next step. Composers who did not want Mouseketeers singing their songs often escalated their prices to astronomical levels so we couldn't afford them. After I approved songs for content and price, I would submit them to The Disney Channel. Ultimately, someone did not approve of one or two of them. This selecting process could take several weeks, necessitating my planning each show months in advance.

We had to have a concept for each number, the production of which included specially built sets, individually designed costumes, and intricate props. I worked with the head of the music division and David Seeger to conceptualize each number, which the music head then put on paper. Then I figured out how to sell the concept to The Disney Channel. After we had their approval, sets and costumes were designed while an orchestra was recording the tracks. If we ever presented a shot in which the lip-sync was not perfect, we would either replace the shot or re-shoot the entire number.

After all these preparations, we would finally record—I always tried to attend the recording sessions. With even the most talented young person, there could be an occasional badly sung note or notes. However, that did not ruin a performance because of the sound technology at our disposal. I had one person on staff whose main role was to supervise an audio engineer so, for instance, a high note that was not reached could be made to sound as if it were. It was an amazing feat. If you can't sing, you would be amazed to hear how good we could make you sound.

Following all approvals, the number would be shot. That did not mean, though, Disney was done initiating changes. I remember one number with an elaborate set involving boxes. I learned shortly before taping that a Disney executive disapproved of the set because it "seemed Nazi-like." We were all in disbelief. Because none of us agreed with him, we went ahead and spent a precious hour taping the number. Nevertheless, we eventually had to redesign the set and retape the entire number. It was maddening!

COMEDY SKETCHES

The approval process was the same for comedy sketches. Each concept needed the go-ahead, and often a complete sketch was not approved after taping because "Stephen did not find it funny." Stephen was the accountant-turned-creative-executive. Yet Stephen was the boss, and our job was to tickle Stephen's funny bone. Not only did I have to deal with Stephen's prejudices, mood swings, and sometimes arbitrary decisions, but also with writers who tended to be highly protective of their material. If someone were critical of a sketch, the writers would pout—typical writer behavior, and I can say that because, as a comedy writer, I can *vaguely* remember pouting once or twice in my career. Sometimes I acted as a mediator between the executive and the writers, going from side to side, asking for concessions until both sides agreed. If the show were taped in New York or Los Angeles, such belligerence on the part of a writer would have been cause for termination. However, since we were in Orlando, and writers were not lining up to work in mid-Florida, firing was not an option. Besides, they were a great group of guys, and one woman, who had a tremendous esprit de corps. Handling their whining and massaging their damaged egos was just part of my job.

By the way, my favorite sketch note from Disney was one regarding a line in which one character says to another, "You're a real rat, you know that?" The note said: "Can't do it...gets too close." The executive who wrote that note was afraid that even a rat joke would infuriate his boss, the world's most famous rodent, Mickey Mouse. It was as though this symbol of the company had been deified into a God-like creature.

REALITY SEGMENTS

Every idea in the reality segments also had to be accepted "upstairs." Power struggles existed at all levels. One particular incident remains embedded in my memory. We had sent a viewer and Mouseketeer to Costa Rica to experience the rain forest. The result was a wonderful piece teaching the importance of these forests for the potential life-saving medications they could produce. Margie and I saw the completed tape as soon as it arrived at my office and were delighted with the results. However, the Disney executive who was usually onsite was annoyed that we did not wait for her to view the tape. Therefore, when I handed her the tape and said, "It's terrific," she replied, "It's not terrific unless *I* say it's terrific."

I have wonderful and also chilling memories of my three years as executive producer of *Mickey Mouse Club*. Although I was proud of its success, I am still amazed and thrilled that my 1990s version has also become a classic in its own right. This was because of its legion of fans, and because it introduced some of the biggest teen stars of the present era, including *NSYNC members JC Chasez and Justin Timberlake, Britney Spears, former star of TV's *Felicity,* Keri Russell, and Christina Aguilera. It is rare that I meet someone in his twenties who does not have a story about running home to watch *Mickey Mouse Club,* just as I would run home to watch it in the fifties. Life had come full circle.

7
A CAREER AS A NON-FICTION PRODUCER

WHY DO YOU WANT TO BECOME A PRODUCER?

As with every other profession, the motivations for becoming a producer are numerous. For those who just like the concept or idea of being a producer, all it takes is a printed business card that reads, for example, "Biff Sanders Productions," with a subheading of "Biff Sanders, Executive Producer." It's that simple. No degree is necessary, no state or national exam, no requirement to have the title bestowed upon you by a council of your peers. All you need is a trip to the printer; and the more money you invest, the prettier and more impressive your card will be. If your only purpose is driven by ego and your need to impress, you will find plenty of gullible people to look at your card and satisfy those urges. I congratulate you and wish you and your chosen business card well. In Los Angeles, the card might also help your social life, particularly with anyone of the opposite sex who is naïve enough to believe what is printed on a business card.

However, anyone who has any sophistication is aware that nearly *everyone* in Los Angeles is tied to *the business* in some way. I have met and even been treated by physicians who have invested in pilots. On numerous occasions, I found myself sitting in a doctor's examination room trying to explain my medical complaint while the doctor told me about a pilot he had conceptualized, his title on the show, and the executives who had shown interest in it. Television/film is the top industry in Los Angeles. It's like gambling in Las Vegas—it's the thing to do!

I never stopped being amused by the *hustle* that went on between nearly any two individuals regarding new television and film projects. In a real city, doctors are doctors, lawyers are lawyers, and bricklayers are bricklayers. Not in Los Angeles! We have all heard the line, "But what I really want to do is direct!" It's usually said as a joke—but it is also said in totally seriousness. I found myself chuckling regularly because I felt as though I were playing out a real-life scene from Robert Altman's film *The Player* or a sketch from *Saturday Night Live.*

Not only does everyone want to be a producer or director, but I also found most people—doctors in particular—want to be *talent*—the person on camera. When I was producing a successful talk/magazine program, my sinus doctor would pitch segments that he could do on the show. Since he was a good friend of the host—and had a piece of gauze wrapped around my tongue and a laryngoscope down my throat—I found myself nodding yes to his suggestions, which is how he appeared on the show several times. He also took pride in the number of celebrities he treated. It was truly "inspirational" to know that the hand on my sinuses also touched the sinuses of Johnny Mathis and Natalie Wood. The doctor's photo gallery of celebrity clients was further proof that the lure of television producing and the power it wields can be a dangerous aphrodisiac. By the way, in the case of this sinus doctor, his desire to be part of "the Hollywood crowd" led in part to the destruction of his life and career. His career as a talented surgeon and capable physician was cut short when he had a devastating stroke at age fifty-two because of cocaine overdose.

I believe my reasons for wanting to become a producer were appropriate. I will tell you what drove me, so that you can compare your motivations and behavior patterns with mine. I had enjoyed "putting on shows" since I was fourteen and had to take over for the dramatics counselor at the day camp where I worked as an equipment manager. I was already a television and theater historian (not conducive to making many friends among my peers), had a strong background in dramatic literature, and had an "itching" to use my imaginative juices to direct the plays I read. I wanted a venue to create real productions. The dramatics counselor's absence led to my producing, directing, adapting, and even acting Captain Hook in a production of the musical version of *Peter Pan*. Working with a cast of thirty youngsters, I presented a polished production to the community in the Crown Heights section of Brooklyn. We filled a 1,400-seat auditorium for several performances.

As a result, I was given a Vacation Playground license and became the youngest teacher in the history of New York City. I continued in this job until I graduated from Brooklyn College at age twenty. I honed my skills as producer and director, and got tremendous satisfaction from becoming known in the community for my talents. I knew that I wanted to be a leader, either/both in the theater and television. When I wasn't teaching, I would attend every television show that was broadcast from New York and study a different staff or crewmember at each taping or live broadcast. Sometimes I would only watch the floor manager; at other times I would watch the host of the show, never diverting my eyes from that person at any time.

I studied TV stars such as Ed Sullivan, Jackie Gleason, and Johnny Carson, fantasizing that I was running their shows. It was an adrenaline rush to imagine what it would be like to produce a television show seen by millions of people at one time. It was as exciting a possibility as sex, and both seemed equally remote to a boy from Brooklyn. I wanted to be part of that world. However, during the timespan of my twenties, my entry into that world seemed unlikely to ever be more than a dream.

Instead, I began to teach for the New York City Board of Education after the Yale School of Drama put me on its waiting list. (I guess I am still on its waiting list since I never heard from them.) While teaching at the same high school in Brooklyn that I had attended, I completed my Masters Degree in theater direction at Brooklyn College and completed all requirements for a PhD in educational theater at New York University except for writing my dissertation.

Because I was a driven individual, I also taught at two community colleges, performed in soap operas and commercials on television, produced and hosted a weekly radio celebrity-interview show, appeared Off-Broadway with the Roundabout Repertory Theatre, and created comedy sketch material I performed at midnight or later, as the last part of an eighteen-hour day. I remember standing in the wings in Manhattan at a club called Catch a Rising Star with people like Billy Crystal and David Brenner, waiting for word from the host, Richard Belzer—Munch on *Law and Order* and, previously, on *Homicide*—that I was on next. Finally, I decided to quit teaching, end the frustration of trying to please my thesis committee at New York University, and give Hollywood a try. I was given very little encouragement by anyone except my father, who empathized with the frustration I was feeling despite his personal fears founded in his own experiences during the Depression of the 1930s.

MANY ROADS TO SUCCESS

No two stories about how people become producers are alike. Some people begin as pages at a network and become known to key production personnel, which results in their being given an entry-level production job. Then, hopefully, they can work their way up the ladder. Sometimes a person gets a start as a *runner*—the go-here-bring-this-there position—move up to researcher and then look for a better position and title at a competing show, which could include the title *producer.* My method remains one of the quickest: Start as a writer and get promoted to associate producer and then to producer.

Another way of acquiring a producer title is to create a programming concept that you could not sell by yourself to a network, syndicator, or cable channel. You could bring the show to a known producer with the agreement that, if the show sells, you will be given a producing title. This is always a risk because if the well-known production company decides to steal your idea, it has more money than you do and can easily knock you out of the water if you become litigious. If you take this route, you must select a company based on its reputation, hope for the best, but be prepared to be taken advantage of the first few times. However, with enough turns at bat, you will sell a show and get a producing title, even if it's just for a pilot. And, even if you get the title only for the pilot, you can honestly claim that you have been a producer. From then on, your rise is simply a matter of marketing for future positions, and trying to sell future shows.

Work results in more work; unemployment results in more unemployment. Making decisions and seeking opportunities must be constant and continual. Those who sit back and wait to see what happens are not the people who get ahead. People who are proactive become producers and executive producers. To be a good show runner, you have to know how to run your own career first. If you do a good job with that, you will be an excellent candidate to be in charge of a national television show that is seen daily or weekly by millions of people.

NEED TO SELL YOURSELF

The Downside of Having an Agent

One of the biggest myths that has been perpetuated throughout the history of the entertainment industry is the role and importance of the agent. Whether one is an actor, writer, producer, or director, there is a mistaken notion that signing a contract with the *right* agent automatically means jobs, guarantees success, and opens doors to meetings with executives whose secretaries say each time you call that Mr. Powerful is in a meeting. Even people outside the entertainment industry, who think they know what it takes to achieve success in show business based on what they read in *People* magazine, will tell you that you need the *right* agent. The concept is that once you sign a contract with an agent, your self-marketing days are over. Nothing could be further from the truth.

Although it may seem that I am exaggerating the concept of agent as god, this philosophy permeates Hollywood. After my first several years as a producer/writer, and my first several agents, I chuckled silently when I would receive a phone call from a friend, telling me he had *wonderful* news: "I'm signing with the William Morris Agency." I, of course, congratulated him and did not go into the realities I am about to outline here, because he didn't want to hear them, and didn't deserve to have his optimism destroyed.

It certainly is a plus to be represented by a powerful agency such as William Morris, Creative Artists Agency (CAA), or International Creative Management (ICM). CAA and ICM were among the ten agencies representing me during my twenty-three years as a Hollywood producer/writer. Being signed by one of them is a wonderful status symbol that allows for bragging rights, both for you and your parents. After all, anyone who has ever seen a movie about show business has heard of the William Morris Agency. However, the way that any artist, including a producer, handles the agent is what is most important for actual success.

Sign with an agency and you will witness a flurry of activity on your behalf for the first few weeks. Calls from the agent during this honeymoon period will open previously closed doors. Of course, you begin to believe this is a permanent situation. However, the reality is now that the agent has you as a client, he is merely testing the waters to determine your marketability. As a producer, if you have six meetings with executives who are looking for a supervising producer or an executive producer, and none of the six meetings results in your landing a job, most likely calls from your agent will begin to slow down or stop completely.

An executive to whom I reported at the Samuel Goldwyn Company when I was supervising producer of *Body by Jake* was hired as a William Morris packaging agent. Since the two of us had had a successful association (in fact, we nearly became partners in a business venture), I discussed with him the possibility of signing with William Morris. His reaction was to show me page upon page of well-known non-fiction television producers—almost all familiar names—who were on the list. He asked me honestly, "How many of these producers do you feel that we can serve? If you sign with us, I can't promise you won't be at the bottom of the list." We both agreed that my career would be better handled by a smaller and, supposedly, more personalized agency (also called a *boutique agency*) through which I could have a day-to-day relationship with one particular agent. At William Morris, there are many agents, each of whom has a few favorites. If I were not among these few favorite clients, William Morris would have done nothing for me.

BUT THERE ARE PLUSES

The so-called upside of having one of the powerful agencies behind you is that it has more clout. Large agencies also come with a built-in threat: If a deal is not accepted and the given terms are not met, the agency will withhold all of its other clients from working with that studio. These clients might include bankable television and motion picture stars. As you can see, it is a power struggle, but you, the client, might become the least important factor in the process.

The Role of the Packaging Agent in Your Career

The definition of the term *packaging agent* is complex and reflects a complete change in the relationship between a client and the agent since the time that I went to Hollywood in 1976. Everyone knows that agents get ten percent! Even moms and dads know this! For example, if I signed a contract that paid me $2,000 a week, the check would go to the agent, who would send me a check for $1,800—a fair arrangement.

That was then. Now that's not what agents want. Even when they did, I was so innocent that I paid ten percent on *scale*. Scale is the minimum amount allowed by unions for services, whether one is an actor, writer, or director. When I was hired to be a writer for Dinah Shore, scale was $650 a week. It was "negotiated" by my first agent. After receiving my check each Friday, I would send a check to The Ray Sackheim Agency for $65—and Ray Sackheim cashed every check without a word. Now, years later, I want to warn other innocents that it is against the law for agents to collect ten percent on scale. In order to be paid, the agent must negotiate a rate that is scale plus ten percent—in this case my agent should have negotiated $715 a week. This is also true for actors and directors, and, as future producers, you should know this rule so you can negotiate contracts accordingly.

Having written that, agencies are no longer interested in these pittances. Instead, they want to have a much larger role in the financial picture of any television program. The supposedly good news is that the agent no longer takes a fee from you. You keep your ten percent, but the costs are far greater. As the "client," you soon learn it becomes less the role of the agency to serve you than for you to serve the agency.

Let me give you an example: I was with a boutique agency when I sold a particular show. The actual negotiations for my salary and profits for the show were not handled by my agent. At that level, an entertainment lawyer handles the negotiations and, like all entertainment attorneys, mine wanted five percent of all monies I would earn from every aspect of the show, from salary to profits to merchandising.

Entertainment attorneys know more than any agent about negotiating a deal that includes the "right" definition of profits, which will be discussed later.

This differs from the agent who wants a hefty percentage of the weekly budget of the show, plus a sizable percentage of the profits from the show in exchange for giving the studio the rights to *your* services. This is what is known as the *packaging fee*. In other words, the agent is now not the client's partner, but the production company's partner! The typical packaging fee is five percent of the weekly budget of the show, and eight percent of the profits of the show.

Incredible, isn't it? Studios resent it; clients resent it; and there is no reason for it because agents play no role in the production itself. Not only that, in order to have the right to utilize the services of the producer in question, the agent can also demand the right to supply the director, writer(s), and numerous other key personnel. Plus that agency collects ten percent of the weekly salary earned by each person placed on the show!

If the studio balks at the terms and demands, the agency can say it is not interested in making the deal. The result, of course, is that you have lost the opportunity to do the show at that studio.

THE REALITY

If you do sign a contract with an agent or a packaging agent, your self-marketing days are not over. Don't be delusional and believe all you have to do each month is buy enough cell-phone minutes to check on whether *he* called—you can't just relax about your career. There is nothing more depressing on a professional level than to call your voice mail and hear, "You have no new messages," or that the only call was from your mother in Florida.

Stop depending on your agent. Go into action. Network through organizations such as the Academy of Television Arts and Sciences, which holds events every month that are attended by people with whom you can develop associations. The famous *lunch* is now essential.

It is a full-time job to attend meetings and conferences, give parties, attend parties, and go to lunch in order to get information about the projects searching for producers. As for any secretary who recognizes your voice and automatically tells you that Mr. Powerful is in a meeting, try to win her over, so she is glad to hear your voice. Perhaps she will do everything she can to make sure that Mr. Powerful does speak with you at some point. You are your best public relations executive; you *are* the product that you are selling. With the knowledge that you get from networking, you can call your agent and give him ammunition to assist you. If you give him information he doesn't know, he will be even more eager to speak with you.

Keep in mind that the relationship between agent and client can be more tentative and insecure than your personal relationships. When you hear that another client from your agency was submitted for and offered a job you felt was perfect for you, when you feel that you are being pushed down in the pecking order, start interviewing other agents. Of course, when you call to tell the agent you're leaving, he will probably be angry and chastise you as being ungrateful. But just as the agent is in business for himself, you are the one who must always make the best move for your only client—you!

Networking

In any of his many guises as the creative core, the producer has to make himself available for the now famous "lunch," which is perhaps the most obvious way in which he networks. Through these lunches (which are actually sometimes breakfasts, drinks, or dinner), the producer sets up scenario after possible scenario to sell himself and his product.

A studio, a production company, or another producer might set up the lunch to discuss an idea or concept they need someone to produce. Although there is no percentage of the profits in a deal that comes to you this way, this alliance can result in a job with an excellent salary and an opportunity to score for the project's executives—thereby securing a future home for your own projects, which will give you a percentage of the profits. Each producer—seller—wants to have a relationship with as many buyers as possible, whether the buyers are studios or production companies or fellow producers with strong affiliations that guarantee production money or a place on the air. Each network, syndicator, or cable channel has just a few producers or producing companies with which it does business. Therefore, each producer wants to "stake his claim" with as many entities as possible. Although one wants to be perceived in a favorable light by the top executive, the producer who ignores lower-level executives is making a huge mistake.

The reality is that the lower-level executive can become the top executive in a matter of months. The fact that you gave him attention during his "lowly" days is often appreciated and remembered. However, if the executive is replaced, he should not be deleted from the many organizers, Rolodexes, and Palms as he may again resurface at any even higher step on the ladder. The "lowly" executive may also jump to the top spot at another company, empowered to select the producers with whom he will work at the new company. All of these people can be helpful to you, which is why a daily study of the trade papers, *Daily Variety* and *The Hollywood Reporter*, as well as the weeklies *Broadcasting & Cable*, *TelevisionWeek*, and *Media Week* is essential. These publications record who is where and what he is doing. No one paper has *all* the information, but by reading each, you will have read everything that can be printed.

You might also have "lunch" with a buyer of programs from a station group. For instance, I had a good relationship with a top executive at Sinclair, which had stations in twenty-three percent of the country. As a result of a breakfast, this buyer became interested in a personality, whose rights I had acquired. After he committed to that personality, I used the commitment as leverage to go to the distributors such as Fox and Paramount. Although the project did not ultimately reach air, my breakfast was well worth the price. Whatever the scenario that does, hopefully, come to fruition, this kind of networking over food and drink can pay off.

Additionally, the producer should have a network of "friends." I put the word in quotes to indicate that these people may not always be friends. They sometimes turn out to be among the first to steal and stab at an opportune moments. However, this friends network does broadcast rumors and truths that have not yet been printed and can, therefore, give a producer inside information that can affect a strategy.

As you can see, producing is more than a job. It is a lifestyle. It is rare that, once a show is in production, there will be time for more than a ten-minute lunch, unless it is for significant political reasons. Through these lunches, the producer will meet the newest executives and find out what they are looking for in the short term. Good producers also keep track through constant phone calls of the best personnel with whom they have worked, so when an order comes in for either a run-thru (an inexpensive simile of what the show will look like), a pilot, or a series, they can assemble a staff quickly.

Just as the price of a stock reflects its current value to the buying public, every producer has a market value for buyers. This means that a producer is constantly jockeying for position, depending on what his or her standing is at a particular time. The producer whose present stock is down must take steps to enhance it. Perhaps a public relations agent might even be hired to "plant" items in trade papers to offset the image and minimize any damage. Or that producer might become totally absorbed in a current project or a new product because a big success could determine the producer's economic future and "heat" within the industry. This "heat" must constantly be assessed, measured, and nurtured.

At times, a producer must decide to "ride a hit" to guarantee "sizzle" when trying to sell his next show—or leave the running of the show to a designated producer, so he can devote all his energies toward expanding the amount of product on the air, thereby increasing his income and, certainly, perceived power in the industry. In other words, the more "toys" you own that are on the air, the greater your power, which means the greater your ability to sell even more shows and gain even more power. The producer of multiple concurrent successes can make enough money to retire because studios and networks are willing to pay him top dollar and offer generous ownership deals.

Finding and Selling New Products

Selling yourself is defined by your product or products. Previous successes can provide the revenue to purchase the rights to a new product when you have no on-air show to provide income. It is during the periods when you don't have a show on the air, haven't had one for a while, or have had several shows that were bombs that you must have the emotional, creative, and financial resources to turn your career around—particularly the financial resources.

How much money are we talking about? Well, you must have enough to survive and invest in a product or products, whether the product is new or an existing concept. Some supposedly new concepts come from other nations. For instance, *America's Funniest Home Videos* was purchased from Japan. With the ever-increasing reliance on reality shows, the producer must constantly be scouring the global marketplace for the rights to shows that have demonstrated success, even if that success was in, say, the Netherlands. Buyers are so hungry for a concept that could become the next *Who Wants to Be a Millionaire?* or *Survivor* that even a success on another *planet* might cause a buzz!

With concept in hand, the producer must then find a home for the project, and decide whether it would work best on a network, on cable, in *syndication*—a group of stations and station groups that purchase the rights to a show—or, recently, as Internet content. In addition, either the producer or a trusted "budget" expert with whom he usually works must "cost out" the show.

Then there's the selling of the show. These days, producers must have a different answer for every buyer because each comes with a different formula for remuneration. A network or syndicator has more money than a cable operation; therefore, the producer must adapt the concept to the researched amount of *license fee*, which is the cost for the rights to use the concept that can be expected from a particular buyer. In other words, when the buyer asks what the cost factor will be, the producer must demonstrate that he has a viable answer for that particular venue. Time is short, and executives want to meet with only the producers they feel will deliver a hit so that their jobs will be guaranteed for a reasonable length of time. The producer who makes a quote too high or too low is risking credibility and may never be granted a meeting again.

All this time the producer must also be reading everything printed in trade journals, studying ratings and trends for each buyer, and acquiring and offering the programs that, in his judgment, are the solution to a client's ratings and demographics. He must also be able to analyze the marketplace and predict needs and trends before others spot them. In other words, the producer must look at what has been successful and then see how to put a different spin on it.

One experience I had with Lifetime, known as a woman's service channel, was when the executives in power were truly hysterical that their days were numbered unless they found a hit. With a partner, I pitched a concept I still believe would have been an outstanding program for the channel. The concept was a half-hour documentary profiling a woman in her chosen profession—everything from police-woman to veterinarian to hairdresser. It was a time when women were returning to the workplace, unsure what to do, not knowing which of their interests and talents were marketable and how much educa-tion they needed. By watching a subject in the context of her job and its duties, a viewer might decide if a particular field was or was not a possible option for her.

After hearing our pitch, the female executive began to cry and lash out at me, asking, "Steve, how could you do this to me? I need a big *strip* [daily show] ASAP or I'm out of here." We apologized profusely and left quickly, even though we knew this pitch fit her demographics per-fectly. Was she shortsighted? Who knows? But that executive was fired only weeks later! It is hard to believe, but the average "career span" of an executive in television is eighteen months! Even the average football player in the NFL has a career that lasts three and a half years.

The homework a producer does includes checking the successes and failures of shows on each of the hundred or so broadcast networks, syndication companies, and cable networks—the so called *"buyers' channels"*—and analyzing those shows to determine what will appeal to the executives. As exhaustive as that sounds, even it is an oversim-plification. Buyers are not just looking for the "what," they are looking for the "who." Consider, for example, the launch several seasons ago of a television version of John Gray's *Men Are From Mars, Women Are From Venus*. The show—hosted during the pilot by Eleanor Mondale, daughter of former Vice President Walter Mondale and host of shows on *E!*—was selling to stations around the country just moderately well. The show was produced through the Griffin Company, known for *Jeopardy!* and *Wheel of Fortune*. Even Merv Griffin himself was involved with the project. However, I noticed that there were few full-page ads in such trade papers as *TelevisionWeek* and *Broadcasting & Cable*—not a sign of confidence.

Then Merv made the move that elevated the show's "sizzle" in the marketplace. He replaced Eleanor Mondale with Cybill Shepherd. Even though Cybill had earned the reputation as being one of the "meanest actress on television," she was still a former movie star and prime-time TV star and could, therefore, generate a great deal of press. Of course, top columnists in every newspaper and magazine had interviews with Cybill, who revealed her so-called reasons for doing this type of show. In reality, no one wanted "to touch her" for another sitcom after her well-documented histrionics on her show, *Cybill*. Griffin was interviewed about how he managed to seduce Cybill into daily production. He reportedly said he told her that if the show were a success, her singing career would "skyrocket." I use the word *reportedly* because one never knows the complete truth. Was Cybill afraid that her career was finished because of her reputation? Did she need the money, a new success?

No matter the reason for a known personality's seeking a particular job, it is the job of the producer to match a name host with the concept of the show. It makes for a "better *package*," a "better sell," if you have a producer, on-camera talent, and perhaps writer and/or director on board. However, the bottom line in the *Men Are From Mars, Women Are From Venus* scenario was the public's ennui. The show failed to garner even a 1.0 rating—only one out of one hundred homes with television sets was watching the program—and Cybill was gone just months later, followed shortly by the cancellation of the program.

That situation demonstrates another danger for the producer. What if an interested buyer likes the concept, but has absolutely no interest in the host the producer has suggested? In that case, the producer must shop for another appropriate talent or be prepared to submit a list of possibilities, trying to predict which personalities the executive will find acceptable. After all, if the buyer is willing to give you a commitment, but will walk if you insist on talent he considers a bad choice, the project must still be saved. This is why the savvy producer, with the assistance of an experienced attorney, always writes an out-clause into any contract with a possible host. Otherwise, the producer's lack of flexibility may mean that he has to pay off the proposed host's entire contract directly.

Now, it is possible that the deal will fall through anyway, perhaps because the executive with whom you are working gets fired or the network, syndicator, or cable channel changes directions over the weekend. In that case, the producer may choose to return to the originally suggested host before marketing the show elsewhere. To prepare for this possibility, the producer also may include in the contract established with the originally proposed host that, within a period of time, say ninety days, this talent can be reinstated.

On rare occasions, a producer does discover a talent he feels will be a *"breakthrough"*—a personality who will generate a great deal of heat in the buying community. It is then up to the producer to maximize this heat, to create the sizzle that will result in a buying frenzy. It is a marketing effort that is not much different in concept from marketing a hot toy like the Furby that appeared in the late 1990s. In that case, the toy company created a shortage that sent every "respectable" parent on a store-to-store quest for the toy because, of course, any "good" parent would find a Furby for his child.

Marketing

I had such a marketing opportunity with a talent several years ago. It was during the proliferation of the daytime one-topic talk show. I felt that most hosts did not have the proper credentials to be talking about many subjects discussed on their shows. Television has a dangerous habit of giving credibility to those who do not deserve it. Take Dr. Laura Schlessinger for example. The public believes that she is a psychologist because she is called "doctor" and because she disseminates advice about feelings and relationships. However, her PhD is in physiology, which is not the degree that matches her supposed field of expertise. With people like Jenny Jones—a stand-up comic—and Montel Williams—military—as competition, I knew I had to find someone who was qualified to do the job.

I found a woman, Dr. Bertice Berry, a sociologist, with a PhD in sociology, who was personally knowledgeable about the "isms" of life—racism, sexism, ageism, etc. She was an African-American woman raised in the ghetto, one of seven daughters who shared the same mother but different fathers. In what would make excellent interview material for the public-relations firm handling the show—which a producer must always keep in mind—a rich "benefactor" had financed the woman's Bachelor of Arts, Master of Arts, and PhD degrees. My candidate then became a college professor, a lecturer, and a top guest on shows such as *Oprah*. She discussed the most compelling and relevant issues of the day, all of which were within her field of expertise. In addition to all this, Dr. Berry was a stand-up comedienne.

I had videotape of her in all her roles, and edited what was, I must immodestly admit, an excellent promotional tape. There were quick cuts of her teaching, of her giving a poignant "sound bite" on *Oprah*, and finally of her telling jokes that received a standing ovation from 3,000 people! I asked my agent to send the tape to all potential buyers to announce that she and I would be in town for two days only—notice the comparison to the department store one- or two-day sale.

Every buyer wanted to schedule a time and fought for positioning. In two days, we had nine meetings, then went to my agent's office to wait as the buying frenzy began. Each buyer called, offering us money to not sell the rights overnight to another buyer. Others offered huge amounts of money for the project. Of course, like good poker players, we did not reveal our hands that evening and let the buying frenzy increase overnight. We entertained many offers and were in what, honestly, is a rare situation—we had total control! It is a once-in-a-lifetime opportunity for a producer.

During this buying frenzy, some studios tried to meet with the talent alone, offering her incredible deals if she would get released from her contract with me so that they wouldn't have to share profits with me and could name their own producer for the show. Knowing that would happen, I had already spent months and a lot of money with an entertainment attorney to negotiate my relationship and rights with Dr. Berry and had structured a solid deal that could not be broken without a strong lawsuit. In fact, I had to keep her existence under wraps for security purposes, until such time as she was signed and locked in to me.

Eventually, we struck a "rich" deal with Fox, who wanted to make three one-hour pilots in ten days. This is when the actual creative work of an experienced producer comes into play: The producer has to know the best scenic designer to deliver a set that quickly, the best lighting designer to light the talent's skin in the most flattering way, and a staff with enough experience and Rolodex power to offer, within a day, enough subject and guest choices for Fox and me to select the contents of those three shows.

On a Monday evening, Fox told me that they wanted to have their salesmen on the road to the stations within two weeks because a competing show from Paramount was already "out there." I would have to complete production a week from Saturday, do an interview with the talent to introduce the best moments from these pilots on Sunday, edit and add an announcer's voice with narration that would hype sales on Monday, and hand the tape to the salespeople on Tuesday morning—two weeks later. I accomplished the feat only because I had already worked with a wonderful staff and design and crew people who rose to the challenge. The show was in the hands of the sales force on that Tuesday morning, and went on to become the best- and fastest-selling show in syndication history. The ultimate failure of the show is an amazing story and will be told later.

8

MY STORY

THE ROAD TO HOLLYWOOD

Finding success in Hollywood is a matter of talent, determination, and not a small amount of serendipity. About a year before leaving New York, I was an extra on the soap opera *The Edge of Night*. My role called for me to sit at a table opposite a woman—what a use of my years of acting experience! Serendipitously, that actress opposite me was Joyce Gittlin also a comedy writer. We spent the day annoying the cast by cracking jokes and laughing at each other. This led to her directing some of my sketches and comedy shows, which were then transferred to an Off-Off Broadway run for three months, and with excellent reviews. When it came time for me to leave for Los Angeles, Joyce also decided to try her luck in Los Angeles.

For months before leaving, I explored every contact I had in New York through the National Academy of Television Arts & Sciences, for whom I had produced and hosted industry dinners and luncheons, as well as through other television associations. Consequently, not long after I arrived in L.A., I was able to get an appointment with the producer of *Welcome Back, Kotter*, which was then in its second season. Using my ten year's experience as a teacher who returned to his own high school alma mater four years after graduating, I, with Joyce, pitched several ideas to the producer, Eric Cohen, which he and his staff thought were perfect for the show. We got our first free- lance assignment, an episode called "Sadie Hawkins Day" in which Barbarino (John Travolta) learns what girls experience when waiting for a guy to call for a date. Guys often feel that pretty girls must have dozens of offers, so they don't have a chance and don't call, and these pretty girls wind up staying at home. In our treatment, all the girls thought Barbarino must have dozens of invitations, so no one asked him, and he was crushed. The producers loved our treatment, which included more than comedy treatments usually do. Most of the jokes that would be in our final script were already written, and the pro- ducers thought they were great.

That was our undoing! The producers and *story editors*—staff writers—have the option of cutting writers off after the treatment and writing the episode themselves. Then, when the show is in reruns, they get the lion's share of the royalties. So we were cut off with thanks, and told that on the next episode we would *"go to script"*—go from treatment to writing the actual script. In the meantime, they were discussing the possibility of putting us on staff—with a sizable weekly income.

That is part of the nature of Hollywood—those in charge pull a dirty trick like taking a script assignment away, and then turn around and make you an offer to become "one of the guys." It keeps the writer off balance. Joyce did not want a daily job, because she was convinced that she had a tremendous future as a television actress. I told the *Kotter* people that I would be interested, even without Joyce. However—and this is true when any writing partnership separates—the powers that be cannot take a chance and hire one without the other. "How do we know which of you is the funny one?" is their unspoken thought pro- cess. Joyce and I decided to keep writing freelance sitcom scripts, while she pursued her acting dream, and I took a fulltime job. Based on my background with the school system, and the fact my father chaired the art department at a top art high school in New York City, I was a man with a civil service mentality in "La La Land."

A MAN OBSESSED

Through Ray Sackheim, the agent who signed me after writing for *Welcome Back, Kotter*, I learned that Dinah Shore was looking for a new writer for her ninety-minute daily talk/variety show, *Dinah!* The executive producer, Carolyn Raskin, was seeking someone who was familiar with celebrity interviews—I had done a weekly New York celebrity interview radio show for three years—as well as someone who could write comedy material for *Dinah!* (even though I had never heard her say anything funny).

I submitted my résumé, *Kotter* material, and some of my comedy sketches. Since it is the nature of nightclub comedy sketches to contain "blue" material, I figured Raskin would recognize I had written what was appropriate for a nightclub and could easily adapt to different venues. It was then I learned the first of many lessons regarding the inability of people in the industry to "make a leap" in understanding. Sackheim informed me that Raskin felt I was "too wild" for Dinah Shore! Me too wild for Dinah Shore? I was a doctoral candidate, a respected teacher, an intellectual, and a person who was very adaptable in any situation. How could I be so categorized by only reading my sketch material? At the end of the call with Sackheim, I actually saw spots in front of my eyes. My hands were shaking. I flew into action immediately. I was a man obsessed. (This wasn't the first or last time I heard the expression applied to me.)

Taking out my IBM Selectric—it *was* 1976—and with fingers barely hitting the appropriate keys, I wrote an intelligent letter to Carolyn Raskin, restating my credentials in my most academic and intellectual verbiage. It was then the man-obsessed concept took on new depth. Instead of mailing the letter or sending it via courier, I decided to drive a half hour to the studio at CBS Television City. That studio, one of the most massive structures in Hollywood, was always well guarded...but I *was* a man obsessed—or was it *possessed*?

I entered the lobby, where the guard asked who I was there to see. I was in a shirt, tie, and pocket square—my usual garb—and carried myself with an attitude that left no doubt that I would be allowed to enter. Without checking, the guard just pressed the buzzer and gave me entry to the elevator, which led to the *Dinah!* offices on the third floor.

When I entered the production office, I again met with gatekeepers at the front office. Determined to move past the receptionists quickly, I spoke first and asked for directions to Carolyn Raskin's office. They told me, and I opened the door to the production offices and walked straight to Raskin's office.

Her secretary had apparently stepped out, so I knocked on her door and was told to come in. I politely introduced myself, gave her my materials, asked her to please review them, requested that she notice I was a tall, thin, intelligent man whose raunchy nightclub material was not indicative of my conservative nature, and said that I looked forward to having a formal meeting with her. Then I left.

A few hours later Sackheim called to say that Raskin wanted to meet with me the next morning. Later that night, as luck would have it, I turned my ankle while walking. Approaching Raskin on cast and cane the next day, I opened with, "Do you hire the handicapped?" Not my best material, I guarantee, but she roared, spoke with me for a short while, and then brought in the show runner, Fred Tatashore. After about twenty minutes, Tatashore asked, "When can you start? It was Friday so I said, "Monday." He responded with, "Can you begin right now?" I said "Sure," and didn't go home. Within an hour I was on the phone, pre-interviewing my first guests, Carol Lynley and Robert Stack, and marking the beginning of a career in daily non-fiction television that was to last twenty-three years. By the way, I don't recommend this approach to any of you reading this book. When one compares the threat of terrorism in the twenty-first century to the seeming innocence of the 1970s, such an act could understandably be interpreted as endangering the safety of everyone in the building and be catastrophic for the perpetrator.

I learned a tremendous amount from writing nearly 200 portions and complete episodes of *Dinah!* I watched Tatashore at work, and decided what I would emulate and avoid when I became a producer. I observed his talent for listening to Dinah Shore intently, knowing her so well that he could intuit when she was in trouble and could write cue cards faster than anyone would think a hand could move. It was a technique that I studied and adapted for my entire career. I liked my talent to feel comfortable, knowing I was always there for them, and could provide an ad lib, a follow-up question, or a direction on a quickly written oak tag card with black Magic Marker, a dozen or so of which I carried around with me at all times during tapings.

On the negative side, though, I was shocked by the way Tatashore verbally abused his writing staff. Tatashore felt this was his right. The abuse even extended beyond private office meetings. When we were taping a show, and a guest did not tell the expected anecdote written in the script (and which Dinah Shore expected), Tatashore would wait until the commercial break, and then explode into rage in front of an audience of about 300 people. Each of the four writers flushed when this happened, humiliated. I still shudder about it more than a quarter century later. In fact, Tatashore made so many enemies during his tenure at *Dinah!*, both of staff and industry people of all types, that he was rarely hired after *Dinah!* to be the producer of a major show.

During the season I was with *Dinah!* there was a power struggle between Tatashore and Raskin, resulting in Raskin's ousting after the last taping. With Tatashore in charge, he did what I later learned is almost guaranteed in a television coup. All those who were brought into the show by Tatashore remained in their jobs. Those who were brought in by Raskin—including me—were out! So the "civil service mentality in La La Land" struck again. I had never been fired before. I believed this was a shame, a sin—something that never happened to hard-working men.

PERSEVERANCE PAYS OFF

During the next two months, Joyce Gittlin and I did another episode of *Welcome Back, Kotter*—the entire script this time—as well as a Barbi Benton sitcom called *Girls, Girls, Girls* (hardly a classic). Again, we were invited to become story editors for The Komack Company, which produced those two shows as well as *Chico and the Man*, then reeling from the suicide of Freddie Prinze, who played Chico. Joyce turned down the job and I went back to searching for another full-time job—until serendipity struck. This time, it resulted in a job that gave me my "producing stripes" and steady employment for the following twenty years.

It all came about when I saw an article in *Daily Variety*, one of the two daily trade papers (the other is *The Hollywood Reporter*) I scoured every day. It stated that Westinghouse Broadcasting, called Group W Productions, was developing a new talk show in New York under the working title *Project 90*. I decided, with the experience I now had under my belt, I could create the perception of the conquering hero returning home from Hollywood. I also knew there were few talk-show experts in the New York area, since the only show produced in the East was *The Mike Douglas Show*, which was shot in Philadelphia. Instead of writing a letter and enclosing a résumé, I decided to be more assertive and proactive in order to get hired. After all, my Dinah Shore experience had taught me that I could win a job by taking control of the situation.

I made friends on the phone with the secretary to David Salzman, President/CEO of Group W, and unbeknownst to me, a graduate of my Brooklyn College class. I said that, if Salzman were willing to meet with me, I would fly myself to New York. When I received word he would, I flew in and had the career-altering meeting that resulted in an offer to be associate producer of the new project. Salzman would serve as executive producer, and two inexperienced men who had been Johnny Carson's talent coordinators would be the producers.

Salzman and I seemed to relate immediately because of our common backgrounds, and his assessment that, my having been a writer for *Dinah!*, coupled with my comedy-writing background, endowed me with more qualifications to produce the project than the two men he had previously selected. I was hired on the spot, began work within days, and did not return to Los Angeles for two and a half months. It was 1977 and I was back in New York, this time with an associate producer title next to my name. It was also the beginning of an association with the company that resulted in my winning more awards and honors than I could ever have fantasized about as a child who dreamed constantly about running his own television show.

I was learning new lessons. One was that I was not simply looking for jobs—I was marketing myself. Rather than just sitting on the West Coast, grousing about lack of work, making a few phone calls (maybe), complaining that nothing is happening, or generalizing by saying that the industry is slow so there's little work, I realized it would be beneficial to market myself to the coast that had fewer competitors. There was a certain cachet in flying to the opposite coast for a meeting— and offering myself in some way that was different from the other competitors. The determination that started at *Dinah!*, and continued with my hiring at Group W and throughout my national television career that ended in 1999, remains my modus operandi for new ventures in the twenty-first century.

LESSONS LEARNED

Throughout this book I have emphasized the challenges and responsibilities of being a show runner for a non-fiction television series. I also want to emphasize the necessity of remaining a human being with values in the face of incessant temptation to get that extra rating point, attract press articles about your show, and "push the envelope" farther than any producer who has preceded you. It has been obvious from my narrative that one can easily fall prey to a sense of omnipotence. After all, as show runner, you make decisions that affect not only everyone who works on your staff and crew, but often millions of viewers. Just as a political leader must make prudent use of power, so must you.

I am not writing this as a moralist who backed away from segments that were salacious, or as a producer whose judgments were always in the best interest of mankind. Rather, I was the young, brash producer who wanted to win at any cost. I have even shared in this book some stories that might have seemed startling, such as my calling the media to let them know there was an assassination threat against the mayor of Cleveland during our evening taping. In that case, I felt that I was just doing what I had to do in order to save *EveryDay.* That was in the late 1970s, early in my career. It was not until about two years later, after two experiences I regret to this day, that I decided, despite the fact that I was a Hollywood producer, I was going to conduct business with the ethics I had been taught by my parents. If my name were going to appear on the screen as producer, it was going to be a guarantee to the public of responsible decision-making.

DISASTROUS DECISIONS

I produced two stories that are not easy for me to repeat, even now. I am not proud of them and would like to sweep them under the rug, just as we all want to do with something that has embarrassed us. Nevertheless, I learned my lesson the hard way and perhaps, as a result, you will begin your career thinking about my lapses in judgment.

The first story was for the pilot of what became *Hour Magazine*. I had read in *The National Enquirer* about a 6'7" man who was married to a 5'2" woman. The man wanted to make enough money to have a sex-change operation to become a woman and the woman wanted to become a man. In fact, the couple's daughter called her father "mommy" and her mother "daddy." I felt this would be great television, especially since the tall man wore a dress and the woman dressed as a man. With some research, I found their telephone number, verified the story, and asked if they would be willing to do our pilot. The man agreed—if I could get them enough money for his sex change operation. This was a once-in-a-lifetime opportunity, I thought! I promised to speak to my company about meeting the price he had been quoted for the operation.

Through a series of meetings in which we decided to try to justify the cost as bonus dollars and expenses, the company agreed to pay the price. In essence, we were paying the family, and the family could use the money in any way they pleased. However, in reality, I was enabling this man to have his surgery. I realize that many people around the world have had this surgery, but that is their business. In this case, I not only made his business mine, but I did it knowing the price was so low because his physician was located in Tijuana. With minimal defense, I will say I did try to warn the man that Tijuana might not be the best place for such an extensive surgery.

The entire family appeared on the pilot in a story that received a great deal of attention from both the press and station executives. After all, the idea of trying to replicate the success of *The National Enquirer* on television was enticing for buyers who were considering our show. The studio audience was amused at the sight of an exceptionally tall, skinny man with bony knees in a dress while his wife/husband, whom we had to call Tom, was in a work shirt and jeans. I had achieved a coup—a great "get."

Months later I received a call from the now-former man, who had undergone the surgery. The "butcher" physician had mutilated his private parts to a state best not described. The man (now woman) was in immense pain and asked if we could supply more money to remedy the disaster. Of course my company declined. He/she then called host Gary Collins, who was understandably not willing to pay the costs for more surgery either. The calls continued to both of us every few months for nearly a year—and then they stopped. I was chastened, but chalked it up as a sacrifice in a war. Talk about trying to justify a misdeed!

MY BIGGEST REGRET

My ethics returned to me permanently as a result of another story I did during the first season of *Hour Magazine*. When a new series begins taping, each segment is placed under scrutiny. This particular situation was about mothers whose husbands had "stolen" their children, and who had not seen these children in several years. We showed the most recent photos of the children on screen, even if they had been taken five years earlier. Accompanying the women was an expert on child stealing—an academic who had no personality. As a result, the executives at Westinghouse decided to kill the segment.

Hearing that her plea to find her child would not be seen, one of the mothers called me in hysterics, begging me to air the segment since it was the only chance she had of ever finding her now-six-year-old son, whom she had last seen three years earlier. After unsuccessfully trying to explain the situation to the woman, I came up with an idea: "If we found your son for you, how would you feel about having the reunion on-air?"

She jumped at the opportunity, and I was off and running, taking the most inappropriate action I ever took as a show runner. With the help of my staff, we hired a detective who said in *People* magazine that he could find any missing child through modern technology. We told him that , if he found this woman's boy, we would have him on our show—an opportunity for him to appear on national television. He agreed immediately.

Within days, the boy was found. He was living with his father on an army base in North Dakota. Like a misguided general, I swung into action. A warrant was issued to return the boy to his mother, who had legal custody. I then sent one of my field producers, a camera crew, and, of course, the mother to North Dakota, intent on taping the moment mother and son saw each other for the first time in three years. A bonus would be to get a shocked reaction from the father, who had committed the "dastardly deed."

On the day of the taping, I received word that our camera could not be on the base, and if we wanted to show the reunion moment between mother and son, it would have to be outside the base. I was peeved and expressed it in no uncertain terms. What they were tampering with was "gold!" Yet I agreed to the terms, since I had no choice.

The mission was accomplished, and mother and son were reunited on camera—with barely any sign of recognition or excitement from the child. We then flew everyone back to Los Angeles to appear on the next day's taping. With the dazed-looking little boy sitting in the front row of the audience, we interviewed the mother and detective. Then we introduced this child, who in a course of fewer than twenty-four hours had gone from a quiet army base to a Hollywood television studio. He was understandably speechless, expressionless, and obviously numb. The drama that I had expected was a fizzle.

Skip to several months later. We had at least a hundred successful shows under our belts when I received a call from a Westinghouse lawyer, who told me the rest of the above story. It seems the father went to court the very next day to regain custody of the boy. On the court steps, he offered the mother a cash settlement, which she accepted and turned the child back to his father. The father sued Westinghouse for involving itself where it did not belong. Obviously, there was more to the story than I had been told. It was at that point that I made two decisions: One was that I was never going to get involved in the complexities of family conflicts, and the other was I was going to bring only positive, worthwhile stories to television. It was my role, my duty—and my integrity was at stake.

During the next eight years, *Hour Magazine* attained tremendous popularity and acclaim because of the information that we imparted, especially in the medical field. We broke the story about toxic shock syndrome, were the first to report lumpectomy as a successful alternative to mastectomy in many cases, and did the first story about the existence of a mysterious virus that was seen in 900 cases in New York City. That virus turned out to be AIDS, and we gave continuous updates about the disease during the rest of the run of the show. When I executive-produced *Mickey Mouse Club*, I could simply have offered sketches, singing, and dancing. However, I was and remain most proud of the fact that I devoted half of several shows to issues of importance to young people. One was the story of children with cancer. Another was having Dr. Henry Heimlich show young people how to do his Heimlich maneuver. My goal for every show that I produced after the above stories was "information through entertainment." I feel that people avoid public-service broadcasts. However, if important information is packaged within a program that contains entertaining elements, your core audience will watch—and learn.

9

FINDING A JOB

$\int$ till here? You obviously have the ambition and drive to do what it takes to become a successful television producer. Now, you must be wondering how to get where you want to go.

There are many venues in which to practice your occupation—small markets, large markets, syndications, or cable programs, for example. The challenge is finding the opportunity.

And to find your opportunity it is essential that you subscribe to several trade publications. None is inexpensive, but most offer student and educator discounts of fifty percent. Not only do they have classified ads, but they also offer vital information you need for a working knowledge of your industry. You will also find it advantageous to know the names of the people in power at the networks, syndication companies, cable networks, and local stations.

KEY PUBLICATIONS

TelevisionWeek–This publication, formerly known as *Electronic Media*, emphasizes national non-fiction production. It is filled with information about shows going on and off the air, and cites the names of the executives and producers who are associated with each show and company. This is your most essential publication if you are interested in the national television arena.

Broadcasting & Cable—Although this is published weekly like *TelevisionWeek*, its emphasis is on new rules and regulations by the FCC—about which every producer must stay informed—and spotlights a different local market in every issue. If your area of interest is in local television or Internet content, this is your most essential publication. *Broadcasting & Cable* also publishes an annual edition that lists every television and radio station in the United States, and the names of the executives who head each one. This single edition can save you dozens of hours of phone inquiries.

Daily Variety—As the title indicates, *Daily Variety* offers a daily serving of information about the goings-on in Hollywood and New York. It is the most "show bizzy" publication of the group. Therefore, this is your opportunity to find out who's in and out at CBS, NBC, Fox, or Warner Bros. for instance. It is also the juiciest update on backstage dramas being waged at particular shows and companies. This is a must-read for anyone beginning a show-biz career!

Chronicle of Higher Education—Many of you might love television, but prefer to remain in academia, where excellence is needed. If you have a Masters degree and are interested in becoming a television professor, this publication lists all university and college job openings around the world.

TVJobs.com—This Internet site specializes in broadcasting and charges very little to post your résumé while allowing you to view hundreds of positions in local markets around the country. Since it is unlikely that you will begin your career in a producing position, this site could be your first step. It could prove to be a minimal investment with a maximum return. Nevertheless, this site should not replace the other journals—just augment them. Jobs are updated here on a daily basis.

THE CLASSIFIEDS

The following real jobs have appeared in classifieds from some of the journals listed above. The station, company, or university names have been removed because, by the time you read this, these jobs will have been filled. However, similar job openings appear weekly.

NEWSCAST PRODUCER

Fresno seeks innovative newscast producer with two to five years experience in small to mid-market television and an excellent writer who understands pace, high-quality production, and the value of breaking news. Understanding demographics, ability to motivate and communicate effectively with staff is a must. Send tapes and résumé to . . .

WRITER/PRODUCER

Can you write news teases like nobody's business? Can you edit like there's no tomorrow? Then send us your résumé. If you can master the AVID, that's even better. Functions as the writer/producer/editor of station promotional messages. Must conceive and craft advertising messages that persuade external customers to watch (buy) our product. This position is in the Creative Services Dept. and reports to the Creative Services Director. The ideal candidate is excellent at working in a fast-paced environment and must be able to meet tight deadlines. Having a keen understanding of promotion and branding is critical. Familiarity with advertising/marketing principles as well as editing, production tools, and graphics is important to this position. A college degree and at least three years' experience as a news-oriented TV promotion producer is required. Please send your VHS demo reel and résumé to . . .

INTERACTIVE SITE PRODUCER

Must have newsroom and web-producing experience. Must possess excellent news judgment, strong written skills, and thorough knowledge of Internet technologies and HTML. Looking for a self-starter who knows how to use the web to research stories and build great sidebar content. Please send résumé to . . .

PROMOTION WRITER/PRODUCER

Affiliates in San Antonio, Texas, are looking for a highly motivated Writer/Producer to join our Creative Services team. Responsibilities include writing, producing, and directing promos for news, sports, and entertainment programming, station image, station events and projects, public-service announcements, and involvement in creating station sales and marketing presentations. Minimum two years' experience in television promotion required. Strong writing and editing skills a must. Send résumé and tape to . . .

EXECUTIVE PRODUCER

O&O in Boston, MA. Gather information for the production of our newscast, and manage the on-air presentation, including show content, look, and live remotes. Work with staff to develop compelling news stories, and make sound editorial decisions regarding content and format. Write and producer creative news segments to attract and maintain viewer interest. Schedule personnel to meet news production demands. Degree and a minimum of five years live news producing experience required. Major market and morning news experience strongly preferred. Solid news judgment and the ability to lead, manage, and motivate staff essential. Excellent organization and interpersonal skills required. Ability to work under strict deadlines a must. Send résumé and cover letter to . . .

PROMOTION PRODUCER

Little Rock, Arkansas, has an immediate opening for a creative promotion producer. Must have minimum two years' experience writing, shooting, editing promo spots on a non-linear format. Special events promotion experience a plus. Job includes image, sweeps, topical promotion spots. Send résumé to . . .

WRITER/PRODUCERS

Country Channel is searching for talented Writer/Producers to produce and oversee editing of long- and short-form programming, specials, series, and events. Experience with reality programming, documentary, and/or a magazine/talk-show format(s) preferred. Qualified individuals will develop show ideas from concept through production, writing sharp, entertaining scripts, which appeal to audience. Good editorial and storytelling capabilities required. Candidates must have an excellent understanding of the brand, and strong organization and time management. The ability to handle multiple assignments and deliver to deadlines essential. Send a résumé and a summary to . . .

ENTERTAINMENT PRODUCER

Are you ready to leave your mark on television? Here's your shot. We're starting a new one-hour morning show and we need a producer with taste, talent, and out-of-the box ideas. This isn't news, it's entertainment. If you're ready to step up to produce a show with new ideas, send your résumé and tape to . . .

BROADCASTING

State University. Two positions. First position: One-year position in new media and production for fall 2003 only. Teach multimedia, Internet, video production, mass communications, media writing, and other mass-communications courses or some combination thereof in AEJMC-accredited program that has good media contacts. Required: master's degree and experience in new media and broadcasting-related areas, is literate in both Macintosh and Windows operating systems with experience in website development required. Second position: One-year position in broadcast journalism and production for fall 2003 only. Teach two-course load in broadcast news, video production, and other mass-communications courses or some combination thereof in AEJMC-accredited program that has good media contacts, can coordinate and produce department video productions, joint productions with Athletics, and advise student cable TV operation. Required: master's degree and experience in broadcast news related area. Send info to . . .

SUMMARY

As you can see from the ads above, the more skills you possess, the better your chances of landing a job. Good writing skills are rare and appreciated. The same is true of editing skills. If you are a college student, make sure you are proficient at _non-linear_—digital—editing so that you can not only produce but also edit your own pieces. Both skills make you invaluable to your employer because you are two hires in one. Being able to edit also gives you more control over your work, because you can edit pieces exactly as you envision them.

Above all, do not be afraid to contact program directors at local stations, executives at local television stations, networks, cable outlets, and syndication firms, as well as executive producers of every show on which you would like to work. You may be writing or calling at the precise moment your services are needed.

All of us are shy to varying degrees. Nevertheless, to succeed in television, you must summon the courage to be persistent without being a pest, driven without driving yourself crazy, and determined that no matter how many rejections you receive, you will succeed in having a successful television career!

10

THE BOTTOM LINE

OWNING A PERCENTAGE OF THE SHOW

Hollywood is a "town" in which people like to embellish the truth for perception. As I've mentioned, it could be that one is signing with the William Morris Agency (or ICM or CAA or any of the other mega-agencies), even though the truth is that by signing a contract, one is not guaranteed anything besides a copy of the signed contract. People drive expensive cars, wanting you to believe they own them rather than knowing that they're barely able to scrounge up the money to make the monthly lease payments. Nearly every producer likes to brag about his deals with Fox, Disney, or Viacom to give the impression of being desirable because no one likes to "take meetings," "take phone calls," or "do lunch" with anyone who "can't get arrested." This is Hollywood parlance for anyone who is constantly unemployed.

Sometimes this need for distorted perception can be damaging for producers, especially when it comes to ownership. Since five or six conglomerates own the majority of the industry, the last thing they need is a partner who has no money to throw into a production. Studio executives would much prefer to give the creator/executive producer money to go away and hire another producer for a lower fee, one whom they can fire whenever the climate with sponsors or the local market demands they shake up a show. To put it bluntly, conglomerates want partners who bring cash—not creative ideas—to the table. As a result, the studios will make a deal that plays into that need for perception by the producer.

Let's say one of these conglomerates offers the producer a fifty-fifty split of profits, a guarantee to serve as executive producer for the pilot, and an option to be the executive producer if the show goes to series. This is a *pick-up*, which is still another use of the word, in this case, meaning the renewal of a contract. Everyone knows there is not much money to be made from a pilot, so the executive producer will be given a low salary for the pilot, with the written guarantee of a higher fee if the show goes to series. Sometimes the executive producer is allowed to produce his vision of the show for the pilot, and often the studio will even allow the executive producer to produce the series, if it suits them.

However, if the executive producer is fired after the pilot—unless his agent or attorney has built in a weekly residual into the contract—that executive producer will never see another dime from that show. How can that be? It's simple. It has to do with the term "creative bookkeeping," which is designed for such deals, whether for producers or even major stars. For example, it took James Garner nearly twenty years to win a lawsuit against Universal Studios for his share of the profits in his huge hit, *Rockford Files*, which ran for years and then made hundreds of millions more in reruns. However, Universal claimed that it was still in the red on *Rockford Files,* and until he won his suit, Garner never received a single check for his profit participation. Fortunately, James Garner had the determination and finances to beat the studio at its own game and won, albeit two decades later.

Remember my story about *The Bertice Berry Show* in which several studios tried to remove me from the package because they didn't want to share the profits? The studios have a sense of entitlement. It's a you-bring-us-the-ideas-and-the-talents-and-we'll-pay-you-money-to-go-away-so-that-it-becomes-ours-entirely mentality. When I signed with Fox, it was with the written understanding that I was to be an actual partner. Since there was such frantic competition for the project, they knew it was the only way they would win the contract. So 20th Century Fox went into partnership with Steve Clements Productions.

However, they decided from the start that, rather than remove me from the project immediately, they would ease me away from the show.

Since I had an astute attorney, who was aware of the various definitions of *profits* used by the studios—some of which fool most attorneys because of convoluted wording—he won an ironclad definition of *profits*, one that made it perfectly clear what expenses could and could not be deducted before my profits were paid to me. In exchange, however, in an attempt to force me to seek other employment, Fox refused to pay *holding money*—money that keeps a producer, performer, writer, or director paid during the nearly one year that it takes to sell the show (if it sells). If I had been economically forced to accept another job, Fox could have terminated the deal with me, and I would no longer have been their partner. So I waited it out for nearly a year, receiving just an occasional stipend to travel to different cities to seek staff. Otherwise, I was without earnings. However, I held tight because, if *The Bertice Berry Show* became a success, I would be a multi-millionaire.

Fox next brought in a creative consultant from Chicago, a friend of both Bertice and one of the executives, Peter Marino. This was done to undermine my confidence and, again, force me to look for another job. Their refusal to put "In Association with Steve Clements Productions" on trade ads, as agreed, sent yet another message to me about Fox's intentions. While I had produced what became the fastest-selling pilot in the history of syndication, Fox did not want me to take my share of the profits.

When these overt actions were taken against me, I approached my attorney about forcing Fox to abide by the terms of the contract. I was shocked when he equivocated. I didn't understand why at that time, but I did shortly afterward. The attorney made his living by negotiating with conglomerates like Fox. The threat to him—I can't say whether it was stated directly or implied—was that if he made a fuss about the contract for Steve Clements, they would not work with him in the future. That would have forced his clients to seek other attorneys and leave him without a practice.

Eventually Fox realized that the only way to get rid of me was "dismissal with cause," which is what played out in Chicago. By setting the host against me for her own personal gain, dissension was created. Therefore, for the good of the production, my services had to be terminated, and since it was "for cause," the terms by which I would be bought out were greatly reduced. My attorney was incensed, and felt I should sue Fox. He believed that I had an excellent chance of winning, since we had kept a paper trail throughout the entire ordeal. However, when I asked whether he would prosecute based on a contingency, he demurred, and stated it would cost me at least a quarter of a million dollars, which I did not have to spend! Besides, and my attorney agreed, if I had a million dollars to spend, Fox had two million to spend; if I had two million, they had four million. The anticipated profits for the show were so high that these amounts seemed insignificant to Fox. Further, Fox could not afford for me to realize any victory that would set a precedent for future producers in this situation. It was truly a case of David vs. Goliath, but David did not have the slightest chance in my scenario. I made the difficult but correct decision to negotiate a settlement and walk away—make that limp away.

SO WHAT ARE PROFITS?

You might ask why the definition of profits is so confusing. After all, if a show costs $200,000 a week to produce, and its revenue is $500,000 per week, the weekly profit is $300,000. Let's say the terms in your dream contract are to split profits fifty-fifty. You would think that the studio would write itself a check for $150,000, and then write you one for the other $150,000. Never!

You see, studios have lots of overhead costs, all of which are added to the cost of the production. Perhaps they deduct the cost of all the salespeople on the road who are selling the show, the cost of the studio's office space, the cost of their office machines, the cost of their accounting personnel, the cost of their legal personnel, the cost of advertising—it goes on and on. In reality, many of these costs can be absorbed by the multiple shows that are being produced simultaneously. However, with "creative accounting," a ledger will show that your show is in the red every week and, therefore, there are no profits. That is why percentages of ownership mean absolutely nothing unless every cost is stipulated as being or not being part of the figure used to calculate the profits owed to a profit participant.

Based on my "get rich quick" debacle with Fox, I changed my philosophy about how to structure a deal. First of all, I stopped believing in the "home run." Instead, I began believing in the incentives that studios are willing to reward if a show is a success. The amount of the incentive should be based on the ratings of the show. Another incentive is the bonus to be paid to the executive producer if the pilot becomes a series. The amount of the incentive could increase, based upon a formula that is tied to the percentage of markets around the country that have bought the show. No longer would I agree to a year without salary. In exchange for many profit-participation points, I would opt for a salary that increases as it becomes more likely that the pilot will become a series. Periodic raises would be tied to ratings performance as well. In other words, studios are more likely to be generous to creative people who have executed their vision successfully rather than being in business with someone who is not on their financial level. However, a small, well-defined piece of the profits could also be included—one that the studio might not challenge or try to avoid.

Many of my colleagues might be incensed at my seeming capitulation to studio fiscal policies, and I can certainly agree with their reasoning. It is a long, difficult road to become an executive producer, and gain the background and credibility to be able to sell national television shows. Once you reach that position, you want to receive the proper remuneration, in the same way a doctor wants to be compensated for the years he spent in medical school and as a resident. However, the reality is that profit margins are becoming slimmer. As I write this book, advertising revenue has decreased significantly, slashing profits for the *suppliers*—those who provide shows to broadcast and cable networks. The key to success for executive producers has become volume. The days of getting rich from one show are rare, both for the studio and for producers.

To encourage pilots or run-thrus, it is in the best interest for all but the most sought-after executive producers to ask for a reasonable deal. In that way, a show that might receive a pass can be finessed into an opportunity. That success then leads to greater visibility and desirability, and the stakes are naturally raised. Success breeds success, and one show on-air becomes three, each resulting in revenue to catapult your production company into a mini-studio that is constantly producing shows for many of those hundred or so broadcast and cable networks. I know several production entities that make fine livings by producing three or four shows at once—a special for The History Channel, a series for HGTV, and a cooking show for The Food Network. Each show has a small budget, but the executive producers/owners of these companies parlay their earnings by becoming production "factories."

As you become an executive producer who sells shows, please consider this multi-show scenario. The overhead with executives, support staff, even studio facilities, designers, editors, and technical personnel becomes shared, thereby reducing costs and maximizing profits. Miniscule budgets might have once been the norm simply for cable programs, but syndicated programming on broadcast is now looking at smaller audiences, resulting in lower advertising rates and smaller profits. Therefore, the cable budget has become a prototype for the previously more expensive syndicated show. You might have noticed, as well, a sharp reduction in situation comedies and dramas on the major networks in prime time. Instead, the networks are opting for low-cost reality shows that can be produced at a cost that is low enough to justify their existence.

The bottom line of production in the twenty-first century *is* the bottom line! Anyone who can produce a hit show with no cost overruns and excellent production values for the price is the executive producer/production company that is going to be sought throughout the industry. Rather than looking at the concept of loss of profit participation as bleak, a reason not even to pursue the sale of shows, and insisting upon demanding what the studios are not willing to give, a new business model must be constructed that resembles some already in place. To compare it to poker, you may pick up a Royal Straight Flush once in a lifetime. If that happens, fantastic! Otherwise, you must build a winning hand one card at a time.

11

IN CLOSING

eing a show runner on a non-fiction television program can be exhilarating and exciting, but it can also try one's soul. As a show runner, you have to accomplish an enormous number of tasks. Yet these are not enough. If you have the skills, good fortune, and depth of experience to become a show runner, you must accept the ethical responsibilities that go along with producing this type of television. Accepting these responsibilities is beyond your putting together and participating in well-organized meetings, making split-second decisions when floor-producing a broadcast, coming up with the exclusive "gets," and taking appropriate measures to overcome debilitating rating decreases.

Your primary responsibility is to the viewing audience who has selected your program. People believe what they see on television, and you control the content. Accept that power with humility and with a fear of misleading or misguiding rather than with a sense of being an indestructible god-like figure. Those powers can be fleeting, so don't live to regret them by compromising your morals. As show runner you will also be the mentor of a staff who will use you as a model for the type of leader they want to be.

I carry these thoughts with me as I train executives, lawyers, physicians, and university students to make effective television appearances. Whether I'm teaching or consulting, I remember that young boy from Brooklyn who dragged his parents to every television show in New York City. Never did I believe that I would have the good fortune of entering that world, complete with all the positive and negative aspects. I am amazed at where I've been and greatly appreciate the opportunities I have had. My experiences have surpassed my every childhood fantasy. I wish you the same satisfactory fulfillment of your dreams.

INDEX